A Village Childhood

Great Stukeley
1940—1950

Margaret Faulkner

For Caroline

Margaret Faulkner

2005

Just Print IT! Publications
HUNTINGDON – ENGLAND

Published & printed in Great Britain by
Just Print IT! Publications
59 The Whaddons, Huntingdon, Cambs., PE29 1NW
Tel: 01480 450880
www.just-printit.com

The moral right of the author has been asserted
A CIP catalogue record of this book is available from the
British Library

ISBN 1 902869 22 2

First Edition

For Les

Acknowledgements

There are several people I would like to thank for their help in creating this book. Catherine Lane and Josie Green for their efficient proof reading, all members of the Huntingdonshire Writers Group for their feed-back and encouragement, Macha Pumphrey for helping me sort out the pictures, my friend Trevor Dean for installing and teaching me to use my computer (and for bullying me into writing every day), his wife Mary for her tolerance and friendship, my friend Gill Brown for her help with pictures and memories, Jacky and Joanne of Just Print IT! for their hard work and suggestions and last but not least, my family who have supported and helped me throughout. Thank you everyone, I couldn't have done it without you.

Finally, I would like to thank the Goodliff Committee of the Huntingdonshire Local History Society, whose grant made this book possible.

Dad's Certificate of Army Education

Gas Company Sports Day circa 1932 (Dad on left)

FOREWORD

These memories are not written in any sort of chronological order and may not be 100% accurate in every detail, for I haven't checked the dates of the events recorded here. I have simply written them down as I remember them from the time I was a child and young adult in the 1940s and 1950s.

Many of the people I have written about are now dead, but I remember them all with great affection (with a few exceptions!) and the many 'characters' who inhabited my world then are as vivid in my mind today and will remain so all my life. I will never forget them.

I dedicate this book to my late parents, Bob and Eva Wendholt, my sisters Marion Corley and Irene Holohan, my school friends, Gill Brown (nee Curtis), the late Iris Blair (nee Turton) and Jean Stillwell (nee Cox) and all the villagers who helped make my childhood so memorable and happy in the village of Great Stukeley, my home from 1940 to 1957.

Character Certificate of No. 5820/64 Rank *Private*

Name **WENDHOLT** Robert.

    Surname.   Christian Names in full.

Unit and Corps from which discharged or transferred to the Reserve. *Depôt The Suffolk Regiment*

This is to Certify that the above-named soldier *is*

Sober, honest & reliable.
Employed as a signaller at
which he has done well. a keen
sportsman. prior to enlistment
he was a gas fitter
Awarded a 2nd Class Certificate
of Education on 22.12.1920

Bury St. Edmunds.   *Eavon*   Major { Signature and Rank

Date 11.5.1922   o.c. *Depôt The Suffolk Regt.*

This is to Certify that the soldier named above was discharged/transferred*
to the Reserve* on 11th May 1922, after having served
with the Colours for *three* years *9* months.
           To be inserted in words.

Place *Warley*   *Worth* { Signature and Rank.

* Strike out whichever inapplicable.   Officer i/o *Infantry*   Records.

Dads discharge paper from Army

1st Battalion Suffolk Signal Section

INTRODUCTION

This book is about the childhood I spent in the village of Great Stukeley in the 1940s and 50s, but before I begin I feel I must tell you a little about my family, their history and how we came to live in the village all those years ago.

Cousin Erwin Wendholt
served in the Canadian
Army

Letter to Erwin from Dad
June 1941

DAD

My Father was born in Rayleigh in Essex on 7th July 1900 and was the youngest of ten children, five girls and five boys. Charles was the eldest boy and Ellen (Nell) the eldest girl, but I am not sure about the order of the rest. The other siblings were Frederick, Heinerich (Harry), Wilhelm (Bill), Wilhelmina (Minnie), Winifred (Winnie), Edith and Mae. Dad was given the unusual and very patriotic name Bobs. This was in honour of the much admired military hero of the time, Lord Roberts, affectionately known as Lord Bobs. On all official documents in later life, Dad is referred to as Robert, but his birth certificate names him as Bobs.

My paternal Grandmother was Harriet (nee Cook) and my eccentric Uncle Charles was convinced that she was related to the explorer Captain Cook, but I fear this is just a figment of his imagination, for extensive research by other members of the family can find no connection at all with this illustrious hero. Harriet was an Essex girl, but I know nothing more about her other than she met and married a German baker, Julius Wendholst, who came to England from Hanover some time in the 1860s. This was (according to Uncle Charles) to avoid military service. This may or not be true, because as I have said before, Uncle Charles wasn't averse to inventing his family history! Whatever lies behind his arrival here, it is plain that Julius became a very successful baker, because we have photographs of his shop, his horse drawn delivery cart (with his name emblazoned on the side) and photographic portraits of his family, looking well dressed and prosperous as they posed for a professional photographer.

Sadly, this prosperity didn't continue, for sometime during the late 1800s, Grandfather Julius, invested all his hard earned money into a venture that he had hoped would make his fortune. There had been plans to develop the Alexandra Palace area in North London, making it into a vast leisure complex, but it never happened and the baker's shops Julius bought in the hopes of good business, simply didn't take off and he was made bankrupt. He died in 1903.

My Grandmother Harriet re-married just before the out-break of World War One. This marriage was one of convenience, for even though she Anglicised her surname to Wendholt, this wouldn't have prevented her being interned, due to her having been married to a German citizen, for there was much anti-German feeling around that time, so she married the obliging Mr. French, who willingly gave her his name. I know nothing more of this man, although I believe other members of my family (especially those in Canada) know more.

All I know of the German side of the family is learned from a cigar box full of old photographs and postcards sent to me by Uncle Charles just before he died. The postcards are addressed to my Grandfather Julius and are from his cousin Hermann, who was a missionary in Africa. Some are written in English, some in German, but they tell us nothing of the writer of the cards or of the life they were leading.

The cigar box also contains pictures of unknown Teutonic looking gentlemen, who I assume to be cousins or uncles, but I have no information about them at all.

Uncle Charles set off before the First World War to seek his fortune in Canada, from where he sent infrequent accounts of his life in the New World. He had worked his passage there and took a variety of jobs to support himself. He became engaged to a Canadian girl, who was nursing her ailing mother. She told him that she could never marry while her mother was alive, so the engagement lasted for twenty-five years, during which time he built a house, literally, for he did most of the work himself. A cousin told me that he had been reliably informed that Charles had made the roofing out of beaten out tin cans!

When his Fiancée's mother died, she immediately married someone else, leaving poor Uncle Charles heart broken. He never married, but lived to a ripe old age, becoming more and more eccentric as each year passed. He visited his family in England from time to time and I remember him coming for a stay with us, even though I was very young at the time and still living in London. He gave me a cereal bowl with Beatrix Potter characters running round the rim. He gave my Mother a silver plated salt pot, unfortunately it had LNER (the initials of a rail company) engraved on it! We had that salt pot for years and we always said "pass Uncle Charlie" if we needed salt!

Uncle Charles wrote many letters to me just before he died, telling me his version of his life and that of our family. He also sent me various keepsakes, including the gold watch that was once my Grandmother's. Unfortunately, he soaked it in Vaseline (to prevent the sea air corroding it, he said), so that it really clogged up the working parts. I still have it and value it, although it doesn't work!

His letters were always in red ink and the spidery writing ran all round the margins and on the outside of the envelope as well as on the notepaper. They were difficult to read, which was probably just as well since he was fond of writing political slogans all over the envelopes!

In 1915 my Dad tried to join the army. His brothers (apart from Charles who was a pacifist) had joined up and he wanted to do his bit and 'fight the Hun'. Luckily, the recruiting officers realised he was only fifteen and far too young to be a soldier, so he was refused and had to wait until he was eighteen to enlist, by which time the war was over. Nevertheless, he posed for a picture with his three brothers, all looking very proud in their uniforms.

Dad joined the army in 1918 and was sent to India, where he served for several years as a Signaller, using semaphore and flags to send messages. I loved looking through the old pictures of him with his comrades and trying to pick him out from the crowd of other soldiers. He and a friend also had some studio photographs taken, in which they looked every inch the Colonial Military Men, posing in cane chairs with animal skins draped behind them.

While he was in India, Dad's family decided to emigrate en masse to Canada to join Uncle Charles, the idea being that Dad would join them when he was demobbed, but it never happened. He decided that he would rather stay in London, where he joined the Tottenham Gas Company as a fitter. He worked there until he was transferred to the Huntingdon Gas Company in 1941. At forty one he was too old to be called up into the services, but since his work at the Gas Company was considered work of 'National Importance', this was beside the point. He worked for the Gas Company until he retired in 1965.

When he first left the army he lived in 'digs' and was expected to marry his landlady's daughter, a lady who rejoiced in the wonderfully colourful name of Violet Pink. However, Dad wasn't as keen on the idea as they were and he remained steadfastly single until he met my Mother.

Mum was a cook in the café where Dad and his colleagues used to gather for lunch and before long they were 'courting'. They married on 8th August in 1931 and were together for almost sixty years.

Dad was always keen on sport and amongst the albums of old photos there are many of him playing football, cricket and even golf. He was also good at hurdling, running and swimming. He once had a trial for Essex County Cricket Club and remained a staunch supporter all his life, which led to some friendly rivalry, as my husband Les and I were keen Middlesex members.

All of Dad's sisters and three of his brothers (Harry, Fred and of course, Charles) settled in Canada, but Bill married Ivy and lived in Maldon, where he had a bakery, like his father before him. They had three children, Ronald, Joyce and David, these are my only English cousins, although I have many more in Canada, but sadly I have met very few of them.

Three of his sisters (Edie, Mae and Win) also followed in their father's footsteps and opened a successful bakery in Toronto. This was Wendy's Goodie Shoppe, where they made delicious cookies and cakes. I know this to be true, because these wonderful aunts would send us gift parcels during the war, which contained a selection of their baked goods, so spicy that every-thing in the parcel smelled deliciously of cinnamon and cloves.

Edie, Nell and Minnie all married and had children, but Winnie and Mae remained single.

Mae was a very pretty woman, if her photographs are any-thing to go by, and she was also quite the career woman, for as well as her interest in Wendy's Goody Shoppe, she was also a fur buyer for a large departmental store, Eatons, (which I think I am right in saying is still in existence today), in Toronto. Tragically, she was involved in a car crash which left her in a coma for some months, until she eventually died. All the other sisters and brothers lived to a ripe old age. Winnie died in 1983, when she was in her late eighties. She was the last of the siblings to go, apart from Dad, who died in 1990, three weeks short of his ninetieth birthday..

Because of the distance between us, we never knew Dad's family very well, although Aunt Win did visit my parents several times and Mum and Dad went to Canada twice (when they were in their eighties). The tickets for their first trip were bought with donations from members of the family and the second was a Golden Wedding gift from Win.

The Canadian cousins I got to know best were Uncle Harry's sons Erwin and Walter, as they have been to England many times to visit various relatives, including the Huntingdonshire branch.

We first met Erwin when he was serving with the Canadian Army in England during the Second World War. He spent several leaves with us and we all fell in love with the handsome, kind, gentle young soldier. I will be writing more about him in another section of this book. He is now in his eighties, still living in Kingston with his relatively new wife Libby. Tragically, he was widowed at a very young age when his beautiful, red headed wife June died of lung cancer. We never met her, but he carried a picture of her in his wallet when he was here during the war and he would proudly show us this and tell us about his lovely 'girl back home', whom he nick-named Rusty, because of her red hair. I thought she looked like a film star. They married after the war and had one daughter, Janette, who accompanied him here on one of his visits when she was in her teens. She is the apple of his eye and has been married and divorced twice, but has no children.

Erwin's brother Walt was a huge bear of a man, who worked, like his father before him, as a prison officer. Sadly, Walt, who never married, died of cancer a few years ago. He was a heavy smoker and the cancer started on his lip and spread rapidly. We were all very sad when he died, because he was such a sweet and gentle man. He adored my Mother and it gave her great pleasure to make his favourite steak and kidney pie whenever he was staying with her.

Walt and Erwin have a sister, Ileen. She has been over for a holiday with her late husband Jack, but I wasn't able to meet her, as I was away on holiday in California at the time of her visit. I was disappointed to have missed her. I have been told that she and I are very alike in looks and temperament.

The only English cousins I know are Uncle Bill's family, his daughter Joyce and her two brothers Ronald and David.

Joyce used to visit us occasionally before her marriage to Jock Simpson and more regularly once they had wed. I recall a visit in 1951 when their son Fraser was six and daughter Jill was just two. They arrived on a motor bike and side car. We have snapshots to commemorate the occasion. They were a lively and happy family and Mum and Dad loved having them to stay.

Sadly, Joyce died quite suddenly after a short, but devastating illness just as she and Jock were planning a prolonged retirement trip round Australia. This was a terrible blow to Jock and to us, because she was a jolly, friendly lady, who loved nothing better than to enjoy a laugh with her friends and family. She had always enjoyed life to the full.

I am pleased to say that Jock keeps in touch with us and it has always been due to his efforts to record Christmas messages and arrange visits that we all keep in touch with the Canadian branch and for that alone we are grateful. On the somewhat infrequent occasions that we meet it is always a pleasant occasion, and even though he is now in his eighties, he retains his sense of humour, in spite of the tragedies he has suffered.

Jill, his daughter, lost her husband to cancer at a relatively young age and in February 2003 his son Fraser died of a rare lung disorder.

Jock has lived for many years in the village of Ellington with his companion Alma. When my Mother was elderly and less able to get around, Jock and Alma would take her shopping, or to keep doctor and hospital appointments. She loved them both dearly, as we all do. Alma is wheel chair bound with painful arthritis and doesn't get around as well as she once did, but Jock remains energetic and lively, running errands for house bound villagers and singing in a male voice choir.

My family owe a deep debt of gratitude to Jock, but we like

him simply because he is a very nice man indeed.

My sister Irene and her husband David and my sister Marion have all been to Canada to visit Erwin and Libby, who took them around to meet up with our other members of the Wendholt clan. Although I have been asked to visit many times, I have not yet accepted their invitation. As much as I would like to see them, it isn't on my list of priorities at the moment.

I am almost at the end of the short biography of my Father and his family, except to say that he was well liked and respected by people in the village. He was secretary of the Stukeleys Cricket Club when it reformed after the war and in 1946 they won the coveted Cranfield Cup and a picture of the successful team hung for years in the Women's Institute Hall (which was the hub of village life) and after it was demolished it could be seen in the village shop, now sadly gone too.

Always keen on sport, Dad took up lawn bowls in his middle years and reached a high standard, winning many trophies and representing not only his club (the Montague in Huntingdon), but the county as well

He never learned to drive, so would attend all his bowling sessions on his trusty push bike. He did eventually get himself a moped after he retired and this made getting around a lot easier for him. He travelled everywhere on it until it finally gave up the ghost and he decided he was too old to buy another.

Cycling was second nature to him, as it was to all of us village folk. It was our only means of transport, apart from the occasional bus. He not only cycled the two and a half mile journey to work and back in the evening, he always liked to come home for his lunch as well, so during that hour he managed to eat his meal, let the dog out for a run and then cycle back tocontinue his afternoons work. When he was playing bowls in the evening, off he would go again. No wonder he was so fit!

When my Mother was evacuated to Godmanchester from London, Dad would cycle from London to see her about once a month, leaving after work on a Friday evening, he would cycle through the night along the A10, arriving early on Saturday morning, then he would leave again on Sunday evening and start work at once on Monday morning. The amazing thing is that he didn't have one of those fancy drop handle barred 'racing cycles', just a common or garden bike! He often said how much he enjoyed the ride through the quiet traffic free roads.

Throughout this account of my childhood memories there will be many stories about my parents and a better idea of their characters will emerge through them. Life was never easy for them, but they did their best for us and we never doubted that they loved us, even though they were unable to give us much in the way of material riches.

Dad was dearly loved by his daughters and granddaughters and he adored us. He would have loved a son or grandson to play sport with, but his daughters only produced girls and he never lived to see his great grandchildren. No doubt he would have been delighted (as we all were) when his granddaughter Sarah in California produced Curtis Robbie, the first boy in the family on 1st August 2003. Especially since this is Minden Day and an auspicious day in the Suffolk Regiment, in which he proudly served, as did my late husband, Les, which was a great bond between the two most important men in my life.

Dad died in the Hinchingbrooke Hospital in the early hours of 21st June 1990, just three weeks short of his ninetieth birthday. Irene, David, Les and I were with him when he slipped peacefully away after suffering a massive stroke. He was a lovely man, who loved his home, his wife and his family. We, his family, still miss him.

Note: Since writing this his eldest granddaughter Louise has given birth to a son, Alexander Ian on 15th September 2004.

MUM

I have said that I know very little of my Father's family, but I am afraid that I know even less about my Mother's. She suffered a sad and cruel childhood and all I know is what she has told me (sometimes reluctantly) over the years. There are no photographs of her as a child, nor of her family. There are no documents, letters or certificates relating to her. The first photographs we have are of her as a young woman. It is as if her childhood never existed, which in a way, it didn't.

She was born on 8th March 1902 in Tottenham, the second child of Irish immigrants William Donavan and his wife Louisa Mary (nee Dougan). They called her Eva Constance. Her brother William (Billy) was two years her senior.

William Donavan was a heavy drinker, who frequently beat his wife when drunk, which was often. My Mother told me that one of her earliest memories was of her Father telling her to sit by the window and watch for the women going by carrying jugs, which meant that the pubs were open and they were getting beer for their men folk. She said that even as young as she was, she knew what would happen when he went off to the pub, so she would deliberately try and delay telling him that the 'jug women' were out, trying to put off the time she knew he would become drunk and violent. These experiences instilled in my Mother a hatred of heavy drinking and drunkenness. It really frightened her to see such behaviour. She seldom indulged herself, though she liked a small glass of sherry before a special meal, when she would also occasionally take a glass of wine. In her latter years she had a liking for the rich and creamy Baileys Irish Cream and thought she was being very decadent if she could persuade a visitor to join her in a glass, but apart from a little bottle of brandy she kept in the house for 'medicinal purposes', she didn't really like alcohol.

Mum remembers that her mother was a pretty, gentle young woman, with curly hair (inherited by her daughter) and she recalls sitting on her lap and gently pulling the tendrils that lay against her forehead , just to see the way that they sprang back. A trivial thing, but all important to my Mother, as it was one of the few memories she had of warmth, tenderness and affection in her deeply unhappy childhood.

21

When Mum was six, Louisa Donavan contracted the deadly and dreaded disease they called consumption (tuberculosis) and died. My Mother vividly recalled the day the nuns came to lay out her mother's body, after the priest had administered the last rites. They made no attempt to comfort her, but pushed her out into the garden alone, while they did what they had to do. She called out to no one in particular "My Mummy's dead!" and a neighbour, feeling sorry for the grieving child gave her a bowl of cherries to eat. A kind deed, but a comforting arm around her and a word of sympathy would have been better.

When Mum told me about this when I was an adult, I was angry at the callousness of those people who were supposed to be Christians. Where was the compassion for a little child who had just lost her mother? Mum was much more philosophical about it and explained to me that the disease that killed her mother was so feared that people went to great lengths to avoid anyone who had been connected to a victim, in case they too were infectious. They were simply too frightened to touch her. Whatever the reasons, it broke my heart to think of that lonely little girl with no one to as much as put an arm around her.

After Louisa's death, William was unable (or unwilling) to look after his young daughter,

So he offered her to be fostered by a German family he knew. Whether or not a few shillings changed hands, I know not, but it was not a happy day for little Eva when she moved in with them, after saying good bye to her brother Billy, who stayed with her father.

The German family were devout practitioners of a religion called Theosophy, whose philosophy aims at a direct knowledge of God by means of spiritual ecstasy and contemplation (that's my dictionary's definition). However, deeply held religious beliefs was not to prove a blessing for Eva, for if she had been unhappy with her life with drunken William, now she was about to embark on ten years of hard work, almost unbearable unhappiness and cruelty.

From the day she arrived, aged just six, she was treated as no more than a servant and was made to do domestic chores before and after school. She told me that she could never remember playing when she was a child, her life was one of drudgery, punctuated by beatings for trivial misdemeanours. There was never a word of affection, a kiss or a hug, nor any praise or encouragement.

She wasn't allowed to eat with the rest of the family, but had to take her meals in the kitchen sitting alone at a scrubbed deal table, using her own knife, fork and spoon, which she had to keep separate from the rest of the family's cutlery; nor was she allowed to eat the same food. Hers was adequate, but plain. No treats for little Eva!

She didn't have a proper bed with a mattress, but had to sleep on a truckle bed made of string, which was stored under the kitchen table in the day. This couldn't be brought out until the last meal of the day was over and the dishes washed and stored away, only then could she bring out her bed and sleep in the kitchen. She told me once that when the woman (I will call her Frau) went out shopping, she would creep upstairs and lie on their bed, just to see how it felt to have a proper bed. I thought that was one of the saddest things I had ever heard.

Often neighbours would report their cruelty to the authorities, but although it may have had a temporary effect, nothing permanent was ever done to help her.

She was often shut and locked into a dark cupboard under the stairs, which must have been terrifying for a small child, especially when she was told that they wouldn't let her out. Beating her with a clothes prop was another punishment regularly administered.

Frau and her husband Herr had a young son a few years older than little Eva, his name was Billy, the same as her brother, although he hardly treated her in a brotherly way!

One day when Eva was busy with her chores, Billy strolled into the kitchen and seeing a batch of cakes set out to cool, decided , much to her horror, to eat one. When Frau came back she noticed a cake was missing and asked who had taken it.

"Eva." Billy said at once.

She protested her innocence, but to no avail, for Frau preferred to believe her son and decided to punish her severely, not only for eating the cake, but for telling lies as well.

She was taken up to the landing and hung out of the window by her ankles, with threats to drop her onto her head if she didn't own up to her crimes. Terrified, she had no choice but to take the blame and was beaten for something she didn't do.

Mum told me that she had no memories of love or affection throughout the time she spent with these awful people. Her life consisted of rising early, chores before school, a day at school (which she loved) and home to yet more chores, before going to bed once the kitchen was free.

School meant that she could escape the drudgery of her 'home' life and enjoy the freedom of simply being a child and in the company of other children, as well as teachers she admired, who were kind to her.

Eva was a bright child and because the family always spoke to each other in German, she soon discovered that she could follow their conversations, but she never let them know this, preferring to keep this knowledge to herself. She never learned to write it, but could speak and understand the language all her life, yet my Father, who had a German father, couldn't speak a word of it.

The family would often attend spiritualist meetings at their church and Eva was expected to join them. One day she was sitting in the front row as a clairvoyant was giving a demonstration of thought reading. Fascinated at first, Eva gazed intently at the funny looking old lady, thinking how strange she was, then remembering that she could read thoughts, she quickly averted her gaze and tried to think of something else, but the only thing that came into her mind was that she had broken a butter dish and told Frau that the cat had done it! Certain that the clairvoyant would be able to read what she was thinking and tell Frau that she had not only broken a dish, but had lied about it, she ran from the room, terrified!

When she left school, she wasn't allowed to get a job as she hoped, but was made to continue as an unpaid skivvy. She obediently stayed, but was unhappier than ever, without school to break up the days of drudgery.

Then when she was sixteen she did something that I think was very brave indeed. She decided to run away. Having no where to go, she thought she should look for her father and brother Billy. She knew they had moved to Cricklewood some years ago, but he hadn't bothered to keep in touch, so she wasn't sure if he was still there or not. However, it was a starting point, so that was where she intended to go.

She waited until Frau had gone shopping, then taking her few clothes and her only other possession, a hair brush, she shut the door of the house where she had known so much hardship and unhappiness and set off for Cricklewood and hopefully, the father who had abandoned her so many years before.

She headed in the direction she thought she should go, but having no real idea, she stopped a woman and asked her the way. The woman said it was quite a distance and advised her to take the bus and ask the conductor to tell her when to get off. Eva explained that she had no money and intended to walk.

"It's too far, my dear." The woman explained, then opened her purse and handed Eva the money for her bus fare. I suppose that even though she was a stranger, she must have seen the desperation in the young girl's eyes. Eva shed tears of gratitude, for this act of kindness was far removed from the cruelty she had suffered for the past ten years.

When Eva arrived in Cricklewood she wandered around aimlessly for a while, not sure where to begin her search. She had no address, only his name. It was like looking for a needle in a haystack. It was possible that he had drunk himself to death and Billy, who was by now eighteen, may not have survived the 1914-18 War, but these were possibilities she refused to contemplate.

Eventually, she came across a dairy and milk bar that stood at the entrance of a large munitions factory and thinking that her father may have worked there and would probably have used the dairy, she asked the manageress if she knew of a William Donavan. The woman shook her head and asked why she wanted to know.

The whole story came tumbling out and after the woman listened sympathetically, she explained that although the factory had been busy manufacturing munitions during the war, with the signing of the Armistice, many men had been laid off, so even if her father had worked there, it was unlikely that he would still be employed at the factory.

After a while a policeman arrived, having been called by the woman, who wanted to make sure she wasn't breaking any laws by helping the girl. He talked to Eva and asked her many questions about her life with the German family, made sure she had stolen nothing from them and generally checked that everything was within the law. At sixteen Eva was old enough not to have to be in the care of Frau and she wasn't persuaded to return and as far as Eva knew, they never tried to find her, although I am sure they missed their cheap servant.

The woman took pity on the girl and could see she was honest and respectable, so she offered her a job serving in the dairy. Eva accepted with gratitude.

"Where will you sleep tonight?" She asked.

Eva admitted that she didn't know.

"Then you had better come home with me," the woman said with a smile. "I've a daughter about your age. You can share her room."

Eva agreed eagerly and the deal was done, so she sat at a table in the dairy drinking a glass of milk until it was time to close up for the night.

She was happy that she had made the break from Frau and her family and happier still that she had found such a nice caring lady to look after her.

Eva never did find her father and brother and although she did eventually try via Somerset House (where records were once kept), she never saw either of them again. She was completely alone in the world.

With the break from her cruel foster family, at last, she was free and in charge of her own destiny. Ahead lay years of hard work in a variety of mostly domestic jobs, but for the time being she lived with the woman from the dairy and her daughter, who became a great friend.

However, this idyllic situation was not to last. With the closing of the munitions factory, the dairy lost most of its custom and was forced to close, so Eva had to seek work elsewhere. Her only option was domestic service, as she needed a job where she could live in, so she said good bye to her friends and went in search of a job.

Being unskilled in anything other than the chores she had to perform for Frau, she was forced to begin as the lowest of the low in the hierarchy downstairs. She was called something like 'the lower house maid', which meant she was at the beck and call of everyone, even the other servants. She was used to hard work, so getting up early to light fires, polish brasses and scrub floors, was no real hardship to her, even though many of theses chores had to be completed before anyone else was up.

She seldom saw her employer, but when she did she was greatly taken with his appearance, for he was tall, dark and handsome with a thatch of thick, black shiny curls. She was quite smitten.

One morning she rose as usual and went into the drawing room to light the fire and remove the dirty glasses from her employers previous evening's night cap. As she entered the room she stopped dead in her tracks, for there, hanging on the back of a chair, was a thick, black shiny wig! She recoiled in horror and for some reason that she never could explain, she decided that she could no longer stay working for a man who wore a wig, so she finished her chores, packed her few possessions and left before anyone else was up, never to return!

Domestic work was hard graft with very poor pay and precious little time off, but like so many young girls of her era, Eva had no choice. However, as the years passed, she gradually worked her way up the ladder from under house maid, to kitchen maid and eventually she had enough experience and expertise to become a cook. This was a job she loved and was pleased to be in charge of the kitchen, with kitchen maids to assist her. She was no longer the lowest of the low!

She worked mostly in North London and her employers were often Jewish, most of them Nouveau Riche immigrants who made their fortunes in the rag trade. For instance, the Lazarus family (whom I loved to hear about) had invented a machine for cutting out quantities of grey flannel trousers in one action, enabling them to mass produce and therefore sell much cheaper than their rivals. They were mega rich.

As a child I would listen wide eyed and open mouthed as Mum told me of the riches they possessed and the life style they enjoyed.

Naturally, they were Orthodox Jews, so ate Kosher food, kept the Sabbath and celebrated all the Jewish Festivals. Eva learned to run the kitchen and cook accordingly, keeping saucepans used for meat and milk separate and made sure that all the many other dietary laws were obeyed.

The Lazurus's had a magnificent dinner service that was used exclusively for the Passover festival made from pure gold, which when not in use was stored in a safe in the attic that was disguised as a water tank, along with many other luxurious trinkets, baubles and ornaments.

There was a set of cut crystal wine glasses that had their initial 'L' picked out in rubies. To my mind this sounded exotic, wonderful and almost as spectacular as the elephant tusks that were encrusted with diamonds, which were among the delights stored in the safe/water tank.

Mrs. Lazurus had a bedroom that sounded like a fairy-tale place to me when I was a child. The double bed was set upon a dais behind which was a dark blue wall. When the lights were turned on this wall lit up and clouds seemed to scud across a dark blue sky and a moon and stars glittered and gleamed. I thought this sounded so romantic and wished my bed had the same magical 'night sky' behind it.

These stories of fabulous wealth were tales I never tired of hearing, but I wasn't so keen on Mum's stories of hardship and cruelty in her childhood. It bothered me that my mother had suffered so and it made me feel guilty when I complained about something I couldn't have or do, only to be told by her that I didn't know how lucky I was. I knew I was more fortunate than her and couldn't imagine what it must have been like for her to have no home, no family and virtually no childhood. It wasn't until I was older that I began to question her more deeply about what had happened to her and delved deeper into her past. Luckily, she had an excellent memory and could describe things in great detail, for which I was grateful, as it made me see what had made her into the woman she was.

28

I thought I had heard all her stories, so I was amazed when we were chatting just before her death in 1992, when she told me that she had once worked on a Fairground. She said that a friend was already working there and suggested that Mum joined her, which she did. They shared a caravan and their job was to sell Hoop La rings to passers by. She was told she had to shout to attract the punters and persuade them to buy a set of rings with the hopes of encircling one of the tawdry prizes displayed on blocks of wood.

Soon after she joined them, the fair packed up and moved to Devon for a week. Back in London, Mum decided that she could no longer work for them because she hated shouting out "Hoop La!" as she waved the handful of rings about. She thought this was 'common' and was something she just didn't feel comfortable with, so she handed in her notice and that was that. Life with the travelling fair just wasn't as romantic as it seemed!

One of her passions when she was a young woman was roller skating and she and her best friend Ivy used to go to the rink in Cricklewood as often as they could and soon they became very competent skaters. I remember a photograph we had of her, taken around this time (probably in the late 1920s) posing with her leg stretched out straight as she held onto her boot. A very athletic pose indeed!

She told me that she and Ivy used to love to join the 'Beginners Class', where they would pretend that they couldn't skate and fall about like novices until the instructor went to their assistance, which was their cue to skate off at speed, much to his annoyance! They would eventually be told to leave and not to come back to that particular session. This innocent fun caused them great amusement.

When she was in her twenties she became engaged to a young man called Arthur, who was a keen motor-cyclist and she would happily ride pillion when they went out into the countryside on their days off. She was perfectly happy and comfortable with this until the day she fell off the back. She wasn't hurt physically, but her pride was dented, especially when Arthur laughed at her and she never rode pillion again. Soon after this she broke off the engagement, because she had met Dad.

They married on 8th August 1931 when she was twenty nine and Dad was thirty one. They lived in the bottom half of a house in Palace Road, Highgate and it was there on 29th March 1935 that I was born. Mum often told me that when I was placed in her arms she was filled with an over-whelming love for me, because I was the first thing that had ever been entirely hers. At last she had the family she had always longed for. I was the apple of their eye and both adored the blue-eyed little girl with blonde curls. I was given everything that was within their power to give. I was proudly introduced to friends, tradesmen and shopkeepers and dressed in the prettiest dresses, with the biggest bows of ribbon in my hair. There are many pictures taken of me when I was their only child and whenever Mum looked at these, her face would soften and she would smile and say "You were a lovely little girl." Then add with a grin. "A pity you had to change."

I think she used to have the dresses made for me, because they were all a basic style, known as 'Shirley Temple', after the curly haired moppet of a film star, who wore the style in many of her films. Every mother of a little girl longed for her child to look like Shirley, who was incredibly popular in the thirties, so untold numbers of little girls had to suffer hair curlers, hoping for golden curls!

A couple of years after I was born Mum suffered a miscarriage, but on 22nd August 1939, after a difficult pregnancy, she gave birth to my twin sisters, Marion Eva and Irene Mae.

She brought them home to our house in Linzee Road, Hornsey on 2nd September, the day before the Second World War was declared. I was overjoyed to be reunited with my Mother, who'd been in hospital for six weeks and to meet my baby sisters.

The blissful reunion was not to last long. What I didn't know was that the very next day it had been arranged for me to be evacuated to the countryside along with several other children from our neighbourhood. I was luckier than some children, for at least I was to go along with people I knew from our street, but Mum and the twins weren't able to join me, they followed some-time later. I was sent to the Huntingdonshire village of Needing-worth and Mum arrived in Godmanchester some weeks later, where she lived happily with the Garrard family for several months. I will be describing this time in the chapter that tells of my early days.

It was in the spring of 1940 when Mum decided that she should find a home of her own in the area, so with the help of the Garrards she began house hunting. She looked at several in various villages, but she decided on a house in Owls End, Great Stukeley. This was called New House (because it was the last to be built in the lane at that time) and was a three bedroomed red brick house (the bricks had a curious wavy pattern on them). It had no hot water, no electricity and the toilet arrangements were of the earth closet variety, although this was at least an integral part of the house, and not situated away from the house as most were, although one still had to go outside to access it. Next door to the loo was a shed that contained the coal used to fuel the kitchen range and the copper that heated water for bathing and boiling up the washing. The copper was situated in the downstairs bathroom, next to the scullery and on bath days and wash days this was filled with water from a tap above the opening at the top and heated by means of a fire lit at the bottom. When the water was hot it was transferred to the bath by means of pipes. These didn't work for long and after they failed we had to bail water from copper to bath with a large scoop. The cold water pipes still worked though. Bathing in winter was fine, because the fire in the bathroom kept it nice and warm, but it could be unbearably hot in summer. The copper was notorious for smoking and sending out black smuts that adhered to damp skin a treat!

There was a long narrow kitchen that contained a kitchen range, originally grey enamel, but replaced by a black leaded version after a while. Next to the kitchen was the scullery, which was quite large, with a red stone floor that Mum kept immaculately polished with something she called 'Cardinal Red'. In the scullery was a sink and a door that led to a small pantry that had a meshed meat safe, stone shelves and storage space for all the preserves that Mum made.

A small hall from the kitchen led to the stairs and what we called the front room, although it was a room that ran the width of the house, so had windows both front and back. The front door was at the bottom of the stairs, but it was seldom used, most people came to the back door via the side gate.

The house stood in the middle of a quite large garden which when we moved in was over grown and neglected. It stayed that way until Dad was transferred to the Huntingdon Gas Works and came to live with us again.

Mum, a true creature of the city, had to adapt to country life quickly. She had been used to having shops on the doorstep and buses running every few minutes. There were plenty of friends and neighbours close by. Not so in Great Stukeley! There were two buses a day, one at eleven in the morning the next at five in the evening. These ran between Peterborough and Cambridge and met in Huntingdon, so she would either walk into town and return on the bus or vice versa. Mostly she chose to walk to Huntingdon, otherwise it meant carrying her shopping for the two and a half mile walk. Even if she caught the bus there was still about a half mile walk up the lane to our house.

The most difficult thing she found when she first moved in was heating the babies' bottles, especially at night. For this she had a Primus stove, which was not the most convenient of heating. She would get the bottle for one of the twins, while the other cried for hers, at the same time she had to worry about the black out and the strangeness of living in an occasionally hostile countryside. She had no adult company and six month old twins and a five year old to look after, with what to her were primitive arrangements, but she was strong, certainly not afraid of hard work and very resourceful and before long she was actually enjoying country life. She soon made friends and due to her cheerful disposition, wittiness and helpfulness, she soon became popular with the other mothers she met at the school or on the bus to town.

When Dad joined us, his first job was to get the garden in good shape, so that he could grow vegetables for his family. He had never done this before, although he had had a small flower garden at our house in Linzee Road. I have a letter written to a cousin by Dad in 1941 in which he complains of the dreadful cold wet spring, followed by an even wetter summer. His first attempts at growing vegetables were disastrous!

Gardening was a closed book to Mum. She had neither the time nor the inclination, but worked wonders with the produce, turning the fresh vegetables into delicious meals for us all.

When she retired, she discovered that she did indeed have green fingers and used to grow wonderfully vigorous and beautiful pot plants and ornamental garden plants, although she was never keen on the vegetable side of it. That was always Dad's domain.

Dad always grew a few flowers as well as the veggies and whenever I see asters, sweet peas, cosmos and zinnias, it never fails to remind me of him, for he loved these colourful flowers, but it is the delicious vegetables that I recall best. No shop bought vegetables ever taste the same as Dad's delicious new potatoes, runner beans, broad beans and the exquisite flavour of the first crop of peas and tiny new carrots (that he called 'singlings') had to be tasted to be believed. I suppose it was the freshness that made them so special.

Thus it was that we three girls grew up in the country, with a garden full of fresh vegetables and fruit (for we had apple trees, raspberries and loganberries as well) and an expert cook to turn them all into wonderful meals. How lucky we were!

Mum soon adapted to country life and before long she was joining in at the Women's Institute, helping with refreshment duties at whist drives, dances and the village concert and naturally, the cricket teas were most important as well, especially in the balmy summer of 1946, when the Stukeleys Cricket Team reigned supreme in the much coveted Cranfield Cup, which they won handsomely.

Although she eventually regarded herself as a country-woman, Mum never really overcame her distrust of cows, nor did she master the mysteries of the bicycle. I tried to teach her several times once I had become proficient myself, but she simply could not get the hang of even the basics and found it impossible to steer straight. Our efforts always ended up with Mum in a heap on the floor, and both of us in fits of giggles. I always felt that it was a pity that she didn't persevere, because a cycle would have enabled her to get into Huntingdon to the shops a lot quicker and easier than walking or taking the very infrequent buses. We girls cycled everywhere, to school, to visit our friends and once we left school, to work, the cinema and to the dances we loved to attend all over the county.

To us, a bicycle was not a toy or a luxury, but an essential means of transport.

My Mother was always willing to help anyone and at the age of 85+ she was still taking flasks of home made soup to 'an old lady' in the village, who was not as active as she was.

"Well," she would say. "The poor old dear can't look after herself!"

Although eventually accepted by the villagers, we were initially regarded as outsiders and this feeling must have remained in my Mother all her life, because after Dad died, my sisters and I suggested that as he was renowned for his sweet peas, it would be a nice gesture to donate a cup to be awarded at the village show for the grower of the best sweet peas, in his memory. We were a little surprised at Mum's reluctance to agree to this. Eventually she confessed that she had doubts, because the people in the village might think she was being 'too forward' by doing this, because after all, we were outsiders. She and Dad had lived in the village for 50 years, but she didn't think of herself as a 'local'!

She worked hard all her life, but while she lived in Great Stukeley she had worked on the land, worked for the Fenwicks at Stukeley Hall, doing a variety of jobs from cooking, cleaning, fruit picking in the Nursery Gardens they owned and even waiting at table and acting as butler at their dinner parties. She worked part time at Chivers the canning factory while we were at school, then later she went full time as their canteen cook. She was the chef's assistant at the George Hotel, until he left in a huff, when she took over and became their full time cook. She then did a good many years working at the Silent Channel, a large rubber factory in Huntingdon that supplied mostly the motor trade. She always fitted in her work with our school hours, so it was rare that she was not there when we came home from school when we were small. Later when we were able to look after ourselves, she took on more hours, but I really hated it when I came home from Secondary school or work and she was not there. She was the one who made our house a home and the place was warmer and more welcoming if she was there.

When she worked at the George Hotel we all hated it, because she did long hours in a split shift and it was then (we were all working by this time) that we had to look after ourselves more. I was able to cook a Sunday Roast dinner by the time I was 15 and although I wasn't always happy to have to do it, I was grateful that when I was married, I didn't have to worry about cooking my husband a meal, although it was sometime before I stopped peeling enough potatoes for six people and made huge desserts!

My parents both lived to an old age and I am thankful that even into their late eighties they remained as bright and articulate as ever. The only time Mum was confused was when she was suffering with a very high temperature and she hallucinated. She would see people who weren't there and tell us tales of things that were going on in her mind, but seemed so real to her. When she was better and we told her what she'd said, she would laugh and look embarrassed. "Did you think I was going mad?" She once asked .

She had a couple of nasty falls when she was in her late eighties and reluctantly agreed to wear an alarm pendant, but this was often left on a table, because she hated having to put it round her neck. However, she was able to stay in the little bungalow that she and Dad moved into in 1976, for two years after he died. Then she became very frail and thin, probably because she had lost interest in eating and cooking for herself after Dad had gone. Yet cooking was still on her mind, for she would dream about making cakes and roasting great joints for her family, but had no energy to make meals for herself, although she still found the strength to make a delicious meal if any of her beloved family called to see her.

She was looked after by my sister Irene, who lived just round the corner from her and if it hadn't been for her I am sure Mum wouldn't have been able to live alone as long as she did. Irene did her washing, cleaned her house and simply sat with her when she could. I did what I could but working full time and not being able to drive, time and lack of transport made it more difficult for me. I was pleased that for her last week in her own home I was able to stay with her, sleeping on the floor in the living room, with one eye open in case she needed me. That week was invaluable to me.

She died on 3rd May 1992, almost two years after Dad. She had been in hospital for a week and we knew she would never go home again, as she grew weaker and weaker. She finally drifted away in a side ward at Hinchingbrooke Hospital with both Irene and me at her side. We are grateful that we were with both of my parents when they died. We know that they were peaceful and surrounded by our love.

I still miss Mum and Dad. They were good, kind and genuine people and I am grateful to them for showing us, by example, to be good, honest citizens. I would like to think that they would be proud of me … I am certainly very proud of them.

Mum & Dad on Honeymoon 1931

EARLY DAYS

Me aged 9 months with Mum

Me aged 3

Mum & me in Priory
Park, Hornsey with
Mrs Loveday and
Peter

Although the majority of this book is about my childhood in the village of Great Stukeley, where I lived from the age of five until I moved in 1957 to set up home with my husband, Les, in Huntingdon, I feel I should write a little about the place I was born and the circumstances that brought me to the village

I was born in a house in Palace Road, Highgate, North London on 29th March 1935, which was Grand National Day (it was run on a Friday in those days). When Mum told me this, I asked if she had attended the race. She laughed and said that she had had other things on her mind at the time!

I remember nothing of Palace Road, but soon after we moved to Linzee Road in Hornsey, and I do have several memories of living there, although I left, never to return, when I was just four and a half.

I remember seeing fireworks from our window and learned later that this was a spectacular display that was taking place at the nearby Alexandra Palace.

Then there was the snowman in the garden, viewed from the same window, that frightened me at first, until Mum picked me up and explained that it was built for me by Daddy.

I think I am right in saying that we only occupied the lower half of the house in Linzee Road. This was, apparently, quite common and it made sense to share, making rents cheaper, which was essential in those far less affluent times.

At least living in the bottom half allowed us use of the garden and I recall flower boarders and a cherry tree. The latter stays in my mind because on seeing a single red fruit, I climbed onto a box to reach it. Mum told me later that it was the only fruit the tree ever produced and they had been waiting for it to ripen sufficiently, so that they could give it to me to eat, but when I picked it was quite inedible!

At the bottom of the garden was a park with tennis courts and in a house nearby lived a child about my age, called Yvonne, who would call me incessantly to "Come out and play." I didn't always want to and it used to worry me that she didn't stop calling my name.

I do have many isolated and disjointed memories of living in Linzee Road, for instance, next door lived Mr. & Mrs Loveday

and their son Peter, who was a skinny child, with prominent ears
. I seem to recall that he cried a lot and was a somewhat sickly
child. He and I played together sometimes.

One day Dad and Mr. Loveday were playing darts in the garden. The board was hanging from a door. Mum and Mrs. Loveday were drinking tea. I had found a small bottle of perfume and
thought it smelled so wonderful that I couldn't get enough of it, so
I took out the stopper and sniffed deeply at it, tipping back my
head to get the most out of it. The perfume ran down my nose
and into my throat, stinging and almost choking me.

Mum, hearing my screams and chokes, dashed over to see
what was wrong. I remember her scooping me up and trying to
calm me. I don't recall how she treated my discomfort, but for
ages I could smell and taste the stuff and the back of my nose
and throat was really sore. It didn't smell so wonderful after that!

Later, Mrs. Loveday and Peter were to live with us in Great
Stukeley for a while.

A few doors away lived the Hunt family, whose son Roy was
about my age. The only thing I can remember about him is that
he would come and knock on our door, then hold out his hand
with the palm flat and a penny balanced on it.

"For you," he would say, which meant that we would be taken
round the corner to Staddens sweet shop and be allowed to
choose something for ourselves. I assume that the Hunts and my
parents took it in turns to provide the penny for us to spend on
sweets. It was wonderful to be able to choose a sherbet dab, a
roll of Spanish liquorice or maybe some jelly babies.

Near the end of the road lived pretty little Pam Jones and her
family. She was the only other girl in the road, so it was natural
that I spent more time with her than any of the other Linzee Road
children.

One day we were playing in my house with our dolls and for
some reason, I decided that my doll (a sort of Kewpie doll) whom
I called Molly had been naughty and that her punishment was to
be stuck up the chimney. Mum was out of the room for just a moment, but it was long enough for me to be able to carry out her
sentence, with a little encouragement from Pam. When Mum returned she found us covered with soot and poor Molly sticking

out of the chimney. Luckily, it was summertime, so there wasn't a fire in the grate!

We used to go to a dancing school, learning tap and ballet. I have an embarrassing memory of the time that the school put on a display.

We tiny tots had to learn a routine that was danced to the popular tune of the day. 'The Teddy Bears Picnic'. We rehearsed and rehearsed it and the teacher told us which way we had to move round the stage. Pam and I were partners and we were told that we had to move to the front of the stage, peel off right and left, move round the outside of the stage, then meet again in the middle. I arrived at the front, but Pam was nowhere to be seen, she had gone the wrong way, so I yelled out "Pam, Pam ! Where are you?", much to the amusement of the audience.

I also have a vivid memory of Mum, Mrs. Jones, Pam and I, getting caught in a shower as we went to the dance school and having to run so we didn't get wet. The thing I recall absolutely crystal clear to this day, is seeing the great big wet spots the rain made on the pavement and the way we all laughed as we ran for shelter.

When Mum went into hospital six weeks before the twins were born, it was Mrs. Jones who looked after me while Dad was at work. I was very happy with her, because she was a kind lady and treated me in exactly the same way she treated her own daughter.

I remember her sitting Pam and me on the kitchen table and combing sweet smelling setting lotion into our hair, then twisting our hair round her fingers to form ringlets.

One day after I'd been spending time with the Joneses, Dad came as usual to pick me up after work, but he was later than usual for I was having dinner with Pam's family and Mrs. Jones had given me a piece of crackling to chew on. Dad said he had a surprise for me and I was to go home with him at once. I recall walking the short distance to our house, clutching his hand, with the crackling still clasped in the other.

When we arrived home I was thrilled to find Mum there, with two babies, the twins she had given birth to on 22nd August 1939. I was so happy to see my Mother after a six week separa-

41

tion and I am sure the feeling was mutual.

I was convinced that she had had two babies so that I could have one. I chose the 'little one' as mine and insisted on calling her Irene, although I didn't know of anyone with that name. Mum didn't care for the name and tried to persuade me to call her Maureen, but I wouldn't hear of it, so Irene it was, with her second name Mae, in honour of Dad's sister. The other baby, the bigger one, was called Marion Eva. I was delighted with my little sisters and was allowed to help with giving them their bottles and changing nappies. What I didn't know was that this idyllic time was to be very short and my life and my family's, was to change forever.

The very next day I was to be evacuated to the country, for war was imminent and parents had been persuaded to send their children away to safer areas.

I was to go to Needingworth, a village in rural Huntigdonshire. It had been arranged that I travel with Pam Jones and her mother and a Mrs. Mildwater (another Linzee Roader) and her son Peter.

I am sure that Mum and Dad must have been sad to see me go and I don't doubt that I was a bit tearful too, but I was also excited, because I had been promised that I would see cows, something that I had never seen before. I knew what horses looked like, because many tradesmen had horse drawn carts, but cows were a mystery to me.

When we were on the crowded train, I kept looking out of the window longing to see these exotic animals, but when I did have one pointed out to me, I just thought it was a different sort of horse and said so and I can still remember how everyone laughed.

My Godmother, Margaret Greatrex, a good friend of my mother (after whom I was named) had given me a toy panda to take with me. I loved this toy and clung onto it all the time, because, I suppose, it was a link with home.

When we arrived in Needingworth, the Joneses and the Mildwaters were taken to their 'billets' and I was taken to mine. I was for the first time without people I knew and I became very unhappy and tearful and wanted to be with my Mummy and my new baby sisters.

The place I was taken to was The School House and it was here that I met the cold and unfriendly people who were to be my guardians for the next few months. I will call them the Blacks, although that is not their name.

I am not sure how many people were in the family, but I recall a middle-aged couple, who seldom smiled and talked to me as little as possible and a younger woman with a fat and greasy looking baby of about six months that they called Bobo (again not her real name)

I was put to bed in a cold room on my own, after being reprimanded for not eating the meal they gave me. The food was unfamiliar and I was lonely and homesick, for at the age of four and a half, I needed the comfort of my Mummy's arms, but no one thought to embrace me and reassure me.

The next day I spent some time with Pam and her Mum and I remember picking blackberries, but I don't recall seeing them again. I think they must have been unhappy in the country and returned to London. However, I had no choice but to stay with the Blacks.

I became more and more unhappy as the days went by and I cried a lot. The Blacks weren't actually cruel to me, but they were completely indifferent. They never once spoke to me in a kindly way and they certainly didn't put an arm round me, or try to comfort me. I was constantly told off for not eating their food, which was disgusting. I was told off for crying and I was told off for not going to sleep at once. I found the unfamiliar bedroom frightening and cried myself to sleep every night. My one comfort was my panda and I cuddled him to me as I thought about Mum and Dad and the twins and wondered where they were and why I wasn't allowed to be with them.

One night I was put to bed and couldn't find my panda anywhere. I asked for him, but they didn't attempt to find him, so I cried even more, because I thought he was lost.

The next morning I saw Bobo playing with him and went to take him back, but he was snatched away from me and returned to the baby. I never saw him again. I was heart broken and my one source of comfort had been taken away from me and I was beside myself with grief.

I don't know how long this nightmare went on for, but one day I was told that I was going on a journey. I don't recall who took me, or what form of transport was taken, but after what seemed like ages, I was taken into a large empty room and left alone. After a few minutes the door opened and Mum walked in. I rushed into her arms and we clung to each other, both of us in floods of tears. Soon the twins were there too and we enjoyed a lovely afternoon together. I was so happy, thinking that at last we were all together again, but it wasn't to be. I was told that I had to go back to the Blacks, as there wasn't room for me in the house that Mum was living in. As she bade me a tearful goodbye, Mum could have had no idea how unhappy I was and I was incapable of telling her. It wasn't as if the Blacks starved or beat me, they just didn't seem to like me very much and I certainly didn't like them!

The house Mum was living in was in Godmanchester and belonged to a solicitor, Mr. Garrard and his wife. They had three children, Alison, Michael and Christopher. They had several live-in servants and some day help. I think I am right in saying that they also had some relatives there too. It was a crowded house, but kind-hearted Mrs. Garrard, seeing how unhappy Mum was to see me leave, was determined to find room for me and she moved things around and found a bed for me in the maid, Vida's room, so it wasn't long before it was all arranged and I was sent for and reunited with my Mother and sisters, never to be parted again.

Recently, I was talking to an elderly lady who had lived in Needingworth all her life. I mentioned that I had been evacuated there during the war, so she asked me if I could remember the name of the family I lived with. I said their name was Black and without any prompting from me she said. "You poor little soul!" I asked why she had said that and she explained that they were a very unpleasant and cold family, disliked by all the other villagers. I was pleased to know that it wasn't just me who thought so!

Maybe they were compelled to give a child a home and hadn't wanted to do so, whatever the reason, they never once showed any warmth or affection for me. I sometimes wonder if

Bobo ended up as cold and uncaring as the rest of her family.

Life with the Garrard Family at Riverside (a big house opposite the War Memorial) was much more fun and we were all happy. We missed Dad, of course, but at least the rest of us were together.

That winter, the river burst its banks and flooded the garden, the tennis courts and eventually the house. The kitchen and lower floors were several feet in water and they fixed up an arrangement of planks that criss-crossed to allow people to move about. Mrs. Osborne the cook, a large, red-faced woman of uncertain temper, was not at all happy at having to use these planks to move around her kitchen. She would shoo us children out of the way if we entered her domain. I was quite scared of her, I'm afraid.

One day Mum pushed the pram she had acquired into Huntingdon to go to the shops. I walked by her side, holding onto the handle. As we walked home along The Avenue, my legs began to ache and I felt unwell, so that I dragged behind. Mum became impatient with me for dawdling and eventually lifted me onto the pram so that I could ride. When we got back to the house I was listless and it became obvious that I was running a high temperature and feeling ill. A doctor was called and I was diagnosed as having Rheumatic Fever, a disease that was common in those day, but quite serious, as it could permanently damage the heart.

I remember lying in bed and feeling very ill indeed, with horrible pains in my legs, but being a healthy little girl, I soon began to recover and once I was feeling better, I enjoyed the luxury of having a fire in my bedroom and watching the shadows dance on the wall as the flames flickered.

I was thrilled when Alison Garrard brought her large dolls house into the room for me to play with. It was a magnificent construction and I loved it, especially all the miniature pieces of furniture that filled each room.

When I was well on the road to recovery it became very cold. There was heavy snow, then a big freeze. Looking out from my bedroom window was like looking out onto a wonderland, for the dazzling white of the snow and frost transformed the garden and tennis courts into something really beautiful.

Then I saw Alison, Michael and Christopher, wrapped in warm hats and coats and wearing skates. They skated across the frozen tennis courts with such ease and expertise that I clapped with joy at the sight, wishing I could join them, but having no skates and certainly no expertise, it was not possible. I was still considered to be too poorly to venture out in the biting cold. Then something wonderful happened. The three children came to see my mother and before I knew what was happening, I was wrapped in a coat, woolly hat and gloves and covered in a blanket, then strapped into a rocking chair. They pushed me onto the ice and were soon circling the tennis courts pushing me along in front of them. It was fantastic! I was whizzed round and round, the cold wind whipping into my face and I laughed with sheer joy and exhilaration. It was a wonderful experience and one I will never forget.

Before I move onto another part of my story, I will just add as a footnote, that Alison's son, John, is now my next door neighbour, which I think is an amazing coincidence. I have told him of the joy playing with his mother's dolls house gave me and he says that she still has it.

Luckily, I soon recovered from the illness and although very thin (for the only time in my life!) I made a full recovery and apart from leaving me with a very small heart murmur (which wasn't discovered until I had scarlet fever at the age of eighteen) the only affects I felt were aching in the joints in winter. Mum was also allocated extra clothing coupons in order to get me Wellington boots, because I had to avoid getting my feet wet.

We lived with the Garrard family for about six months, during which time Mum had the twins christened in Godmanchester Parish Church. Mrs. Osborne was Marion's Godmother and Joan Woods (a girl who worked for Mrs. Garrard on a daily basis), was Godmother to Irene.

Kind Mrs. Garrard arranged for a party after the ceremony as a surprise for my mother. There was a pretty iced cake, adorned with two little pink china cradles. There was even a present for me as well as little bracelets and other gifts for the twins. Mrs. Garrard gave me a slender gold chain, with a gold wire pendant in the shape of a spider's web, with a spider in the centre. This had a seed pearl for its head, a turquoise body set in gold and gold wire legs. It was quite beautiful and I was thrilled with it. I kept it for many years, until one day I begged Mum to let me take it to school to show my friends. She reluctantly agreed. I was devastated when I found that I had lost the spider somewhere. I searched the playground and the school room, but to no avail. Mum was cross with me too, as well she might be.

Mrs. Garrard remained a good friend to my family for many years. She was elegant, beautiful and very kind. She attended my wedding, giving us a generous wedding gift and when we moved to the house I still live in, she gave us some beautiful shrubs for our garden. My mother loved her dearly and was forever thankful that she and the twins were evacuated to the home of such a truly good family. So many people were treated very badly by the people that took them in.

Eventually, Mum decided that since the war wasn't going to be over by Christmas, as was first predicted, she should look for somewhere more permanent to live. The twins were getting bigger and it was almost time for me to start school, so with the help of Mr. & Mrs. Garrard, she set about house hunting. She looked at several houses and cottages in the area, but eventually decided on a house in Great Stukeley.

THE VILLAGE
SCHOOL
AND ITS
TEACHERS

Great Stukeley C of E School 1947

Whole school with Miss Smith on the left and Miss Leppard
with Tommy the cat on the right

Soon after we moved into the village, just after my 5th birthday, I was enrolled at the Church of England School in Great Stukeley where I was to stay until I was twelve.

Miss Leppard (she pronounced it Le Pard) was the headmistress who taught children from eight until they left school at the age of fourteen. Her assistant was Miss Smith, who was responsible for the four to eight year olds

It was these two redoubtable ladies who, with very little equipment, were in charge of the education of all the village children.

MISS LEPPARD

My first May Day
1940

Miss Frances Elizabeth Leppard was a big woman, tall, big-bosomed and broad in the beam. She already looked old to me when I started school in 1940, for she had white hair, which was parted in the centre, plaited and wound round and round , then fastened at the nape of her neck in a tight bun. She had rather prominent teeth and her eyes bulged slightly behind her horn-rimmed spectacles, which were sometimes replaced by pinc nez spectacles, with a little chain hanging from one side. This chain would tremble and quiver when she became agitated.

She favoured thick woollen skirts and belted jumpers with v-necks, beneath which she wore a little piece of silk or cotton material, known as a 'modesty vest', which prevented her showing any cleavage if the 'V' was too low. Her sturdy legs were encased in thick lisle stockings in both summer and winter. She wore stout leather shoes with a slight heel, buckled and with a tongued upper. They always reminded me of the sort of shoes that Prince Charming wore in my illustrated book of fairy tales.

Miss Leppard loved music, art, literature and nature and I am sure she became very frustrated (in vain, in most cases) with trying to instil these passions into the Philistine village children she was destined to teach.

She would have us try to copy her beautiful copper plate writing, but lack of expertise, plus the use of scratchy wartime dipper pens, made this an impossible task for us, although she made us persevere.

She was a very versatile teacher, as was Miss Smith, and every other village school teacher in those days, for she taught every subject from Religious Knowledge (or Scripture, as we used to call it) through to the three 'Rs', history, geography, physical training and mathematics (we called it sums). She also taught girls basic needlework , embroidery and knitting. The boys were given a working knowledge of gardening, working a strip of land beside the school and growing a few valuable crops. I think the Caretaker may have helped out with that project.

I well remember my first knitting lesson with Miss Leppard, during which I got in a tremendous tangle with the dish cloth I was attempting to knit for my mother, with a thick greyish yarn and huge wooden needles. She showed me how to wind the yarn round the needles, pull the loop through and slip it off, pointing out how important it was to do this manoeuvre in the right order.

"If you say in, round, through, off, it will make it easier." She explained.

And to a certain extent it did, although I am sure I still dropped a lot of stitches.

My mother loved to tell of how, on taking this piece of work home with me in order to practice, I was sitting wielding my large wooden needles and intoning my "In, round, through, off." mantra, when I suddenly let out a yell.

"Oh no!" I wailed. "Now I'll have to undo it!"

"Why?" Asked Mum. "Have you dropped a stitch?"

"No," I said. "I forgot to say in, round, through, off."

After my initial lesson with Miss Leppard, it fell to older girls, who had already learned the art of knitting, to guide me in the intricacies of plain, purl, stocking stitch and moss stitch. Jessie Deller was the first 'big girl' to teach me. She was a kind girl and very patient, although I was a little hurt when she showed my messy work to her friend and they both laughed! Jessie lived at Raby's Farm, which although officially in Great Stukeley, was really closer to the village of Brampton and some way from the school, with her parents and sisters, Frances, Flossy, Freda and young brother Tony. Yet another branch of the great family of Deller that populated the village .

Miss Leppard was a deeply religious woman, as one would expect of the headmistress of a Church of England School. She was a regular church goer and played the organ for all the church services. She was involved in most church affairs and would arrange flowers, using her artistic talent to decorate the church for all the different festivals in the church year.

She would do anything to help the Vicar, for she adored him and was his willing slave.

The Reverend Lewis Woolford (simply known to us as The Vicar) was an elderly bachelor who lived in a modern bungalow close to the church, just a couple of hundred yards away from the school. He was a kind, gentle man and much loved in the village. He would take a Scripture class at the school on alternate

Friday mornings. On the other Fridays we would all troop up to the church for a service.

Miss Leppard would flutter and twitter around the Vicar when he called in at the school, ever willing to please him and would accompany our hymn singing both in school and church and her strong, high pitched voice could be heard above everyone else as she sang the hymns and psalms.

She was always the one who played the organ for christenings, weddings and funerals and if she had a new piece of music to rehearse, she would ask one of the children to pump the organ for her. For this she would pay the child a penny or so, depending on how long they were there.

The children who lived in Church End had more or less cornered the market in organ pumping, because they lived close to the church, but I seldom got the opportunity, for I lived too far away and across the main road.

However, I do recall one occasion when my friend Gillian Curtis and I were asked to do it.

The handle for the pump was at the back of the organ and out of sight of Miss Leppard. It was hard work, but we soon perfected a regular rhythm and Miss Leppard was enjoying playing her new piece of music.

Gill and I were incorrigible gigglers and we soon became involved in discussing the latest book we'd been reading. It wasn't until we heard the asthmatic gasp of the ancient organ that we realised that we had been lax in pumping duties, so we had to pump furiously , so that the sudden rush of air would get the bellows working again.

Miss Leppard became very impatient and leaned round the side of the organ.

"Keep up, girls, PLEASE!" She hissed.

She still gave us our three pence each though.

The bane of Miss Leppard's life was Donald Barton (not his real name).

This boy was about my age and was disruptive both in school and out.

He was the only child of a couple living in Owls End. His father was in the army, so Donald was utterly spoiled by his mother, who adored him and could see no wrong in him.

Donald left school unable to read or write and I can remember feeling great pity for him when I was asking everyone in the school to sign my new autograph album and when I asked him to do so he had to ask me how to spell his name. That struck me as being awful, for I got such great pleasure from reading, that I couldn't contemplate life without this skill.

I don't think it was the fault of either Miss Smith or Miss Leppard, because every other child could read by the time they entered The Big Room (Miss Leppard's domain). In this day and age Donald would probably be called dyslectic and suffering from Attention Deficiency Syndrome, but back then he was simply a 'bad boy', which he undoubtedly was !

Donald was violent, a liar and disobedient. He swore and bullied younger children and disrupted many lessons.

On the rare occasions a boy had transgressed to the point where Miss Leppard considered that corporal punishment was the only course of action, the whole school was assembled in the Big Room in order to witness the ritual.

The sinner was brought before us, then Miss Leppard, cane in hand, would tell us in grave tones about the crime that had been committed and the punishment deemed necessary by her. The boy was then required to bend across her knee as she sat in her chair, while she administered the number of strokes to which he had been sentenced to his backside.

Well, that was the theory. Unfortunately, some of the sinners had other ideas and it was not unknown for a tussle to break out, as the reluctant boy fought against having to accept his punishment.

I can remember several exciting occasions when an actual chase took place, with Miss Leppard (surprisingly agile for such a large and elderly lady) pursuing the culprit round the room, and on one never to be forgotten day, the garden, administering the strokes he had been sentenced to in any way she could manage, even if it was on the run!

This was not a very dignified procedure for either boy or teacher, but justice had to be seen to be done.

I assume that this public form of corporal punishment was

meant to be a deterrent and it must have worked, for I don't think it happened very often and only to two boys in my memory. Donald Barton and a much older lad, just before he left school.

Girls were never caned, but Miss Leppard had other ways of punishing any females who stepped out of line. We were given lines to write, or pieces of the bible to copy and memorise. Sometimes we had to help clean out a cupboard, or some other chore within the school.

Each punishment was entered into what Miss Leppard called the Punishment Book, with the date it took place and the crime that had brought it about, so that when the School Inspector came to call, he could see who had offended and what punishment had been meted out.

I am happy to say that my name never appeared in The Punishment Book, for although I was no angel, my 'crimes' were of a lesser nature and didn't require recording. Although one day I did commit a misdemeanour that might have earned me an entry.

I was looking for something in one of the supply cupboards and found a wonderful paintbrush. It had long silky hairs that came to a point and a slender maroon handle, with the word 'sable' embossed in gold. It was beautiful and not in the least like the plain wooden handled, spiky brushes that were available in those wartime days, that were so stiff and rigid that it was impossible to paint without going over the edges. I couldn't believe my luck and reasoned that it must have been there a long time, and hadn't been used, so it must be all right for me to take it home.

I slipped it into my pocket and carried it home in triumph.

When I showed it to my mother, the following conversation took place.

Me: Look at this lovely paint brush I found.

Mum: Where did you find it?

Me: In a cupboard.

Mum: So you found it before it was lost, did you?

Me: I suppose so.

Mum: Did you tell Miss Leppard about it?

Me: No.

Mum: So you didn't ask if you could have it?

Me: No.

Mum: Don't you think that's stealing?

Me: But it doesn't belong to anyone.

Mum: Yes, it does. It belongs to the school. What have I told you about stealing? I'm ashamed of you.

Me: (feeling really guilty) Sorry, Mum, but …

Mum: No, buts! This is what you'll do tomorrow. Take the brush to Miss Leppard and say "I'm sorry, but I stole this brush." Now, don't you forget to do just as I say. I shall ask her when I collect you from school tomorrow afternoon, so you had better not try and slip it back in the cupboard without telling her. Is that understood?

She didn't say anything else about it, but I knew she meant what she said, so I took the brush to Miss Leppard and confessed.

She looked very solemn as she took it from me and said that since I had seen the error of my ways she wouldn't punish me any more, as she was sure I had learned my lesson.

I wasn't allowed to take the brush home with me, as I had hoped, but I was given it to use when we painted in school. I certainly learned my lesson and I never stole anything from school again.

Miss Leppard was very fond of needlework, which she thought every girl should learn to do, so we made things for our mothers from the selection of materials she had. We made lavender bags from the lavender flowers we harvested every summer from the front border of the school. We embroidered iron holders, peg bags, spectacles cases and handkerchiefs.

All had our mothers initials emblazoned across them in cross stitch. Later we learned how to do more complicated stitches, like lazy daisy, stem and satin stitch. This was the only form of needlework I liked and can still make a good job of embroidering designs onto pillow slips, cushion covers, table cloths and the like, but mundane things like hemming and seams are something I never quite mastered.

Every Christmas the Big Room had a large Christmas Tree standing in one corner, which we decorated with paper chains and pieces of tinsel and any other baubles and bits and pieces we could salvage from home.

Miss Leppard always placed a present for every child in the school under the tree … and every year it was the same thing … a carefully wrapped and labelled daffodil or hyacinth bulb. As an adult, I would have loved to receive such a gift, but as a child it seemed to be the most boring of presents one could imagine! We were unable to appreciate the beauty and wonder stored in each of the dried and uninteresting looking bulbs. These little parcels were dished out to us at the end of term party, taken home and forgotten about!

Much more exciting were the Canadian/American Red Cross parcels that we received. These were white and about the size of a shoe box, emblazoned with a red cross on the lid. Inside were all kinds of wonderful things sent to English children from the much less deprived children from across the Atlantic.

They might contain a little bag of marbles, some crayons, pencils and drawing paper. There was probably a bar of chocolate, some Chinese Checkers, a little doll or if it were for a boy a toy car or boat. A little tablet of scented soap was a real luxury, but my favourites were the books of cardboard cut out dolls that came with a whole wardrobe of paper clothes to fit on them with little hinges.

I wish I could thank (even now) the children and their parents who made up these magical boxes for the deprived wartime children in Great Britain. They brought us great joy.

Without fail when we returned to school in the new year, Miss Leppard would tell us just how much she had spent on the bulbs (emphasising that it was from her own pocket!), adding that she didn't expect any of us had actually planted them, because we were ungrateful children who didn't deserve to be given something as wonderful as a bulb, which she couldn't really afford. We used to think to ourselves, don't bother then, we don't like your rotten old bulbs anyway!, because we were cruel and inconsiderate children and didn't deserve so generous a teacher!

I think Miss Leppard must have been a lonely lady, because she didn't really mix with the village people and appeared to have no real friends. However, she would regale us children with stories about things that my mother found fascinating.

For instance, she told us that we weren't to assume that just because she wasn't married, she had never been asked. She said that when she was young she had no less than ten proposals, but she had turned them all down in order to devote her life to us, but naturally, she added, we didn't appreciate this sacrifice, because we were ungrateful children who didn't deserve her.

She also told us that when she was a young girl, she was beautiful and had waist length golden hair. We found this very difficult to believe, because for one thing we couldn't ever envisage her being beautiful and for another, we couldn't envisage her being young!

Miss Leppard was, I am sure, well past retirement age, but it being wartime, many teachers stayed at their posts, while the younger ones served in the forces. Miss Leppard was happy to do so, but then a traumatic event happened that really upset her and turned her life upside down.

The Vicar, who lived alone , except for his green parrot Arthur, and was in poor health, decided to employ a housekeeper. Miss Warne (a newcomer to the village) was a sweet natured and gentle lady, but poor Miss Leppard was outraged at her intrusion into her beloved Vicar's life.

Miss Warne was probably no older than fifty, considerably younger than Miss Leppard and she took over many of the church duties that our teacher had performed with such devotion. For instance, she played the organ for church services, she arranged the flowers and looked after the Vicar's every comfort. Miss Leppard felt left out in the cold and neglected by him and made no bones about letting the children in her care know about it.

She would openly criticise everything Miss Warne did. She would be close to tears as she related to us her hurt and rejection.

When Miss Warne decorated the Christmas Tree that always stood on the chancel steps, it was the last straw. Miss Leppard assembled all the school and declared that she had been insulted, because for years she had used her own decorations, baubles and stars that had been in her family for years, yet now, without so much as a by your leave, a newcomer had taken over this task. Her face was red, her eyes bulged and her pince-nez quivered as she shook with rage and indignation. She talked about people being ungrateful for all she had done in the past, then fled from the room and went to her house.

Miss Smith eventually persuaded her to return, but she was never the same again. I am sure the poor Vicar had no idea of the hurt he had caused his faithful friend, for he was ill with cancer of the stomach, he was old and frail and needed someone to look after him. I am sure he felt that Miss Leppard would be grateful for someone to take over a few of her duties, for she too, was far from young. However, being a bachelor and unused to the ways of women, he just didn't realise how unhappy he had made her by taking away the only interests she had outside of her teaching career.

She had no one else to confide in, so she simply let all her emotions flow out to the children in her school. Unfortunately, she could have drawn little comfort from our response to her plight, because we simply wondered what all the fuss was about!

She still attended church, but she no longer played the organ or performed any of the duties she once enjoyed, and when the Vicar visited the school, she no longer fussed around him, but was cold and distant.

The tragedy of this basically well-meaning and generous teacher was that she was fated to spend her life in the service of others without any real thanks. She remained remote and undoubtedly lonely and I doubt if she ever uttered a frivolous remark in her whole life! If she had a sense of humour then she kept it well hidden and never exposed it to the many children she taught throughout her long career. However, we all have reason to be grateful to her, for with little or no equipment and with only Miss Smith to assist her, she taught children of all ages the basics of education.

Her retirement when it came was a complete surprise, for she burst into assembly one day , looking red eyed and furious.

"You've got your way at last, Barton!" She cried. "The doctor has ordered me to retire and it is all your fault!"

We all gazed at the defiant Donald and wondered what new

atrocity he had committed to make our teacher so ill. It turned out that it was nothing, just the stress of teaching a class of children of varying ages and abilities and the depression of being displaced in the Vicar's life by the charming and sweet Miss Warne. It had all been too much for her. Donald had given her many problems, but I think it was unfair of her to blame him entirely

It was now 1947 and even in the back water of Great Stukeley, things were changing rapidly. The Secondary Modern School had been set up and my good friend Iris Turton and I were to be the first of the children to go to the one in Huntingdon in the autumn of that year. Miss Leppard had had her day and the time had come for her to leave the teaching profession.

I can remember no big social gathering to send her on her way and neither can I recall a presentation of any kind. To my mind she simply just stopped coming to the school.

She continued to live in the wooden bungalow she had occupied for some years and spent her days gardening, playing the piano and reading. She remained as aloof and remote in retirement as she had whilst teaching.

Miss Leppard was a strange and eccentric woman, but she did a difficult job to the best of her ability. She had little in the way of resources, but she managed to instil in me a desire to learn, a love of poetry (we had to learn them by heart) and I could still knit a dishcloth if asked!

She had a real talent for reading aloud, making the characters in the books come alive. The little classroom was still and silent as we hung on her every word as we learned about "The Children of the New Forest", "Little Lord Fauntleroy" and "Black Beauty".

Many years later on my wedding day, I received a pretty card with a two and sixpenny savings stamp enclosed. Inside were the words, written in immaculate copperplate hand writing, "From a Friend, wishing you much happiness." There was no signature. I was very touched by this 'anonymous' gift (that could only have come from my old teacher!) Perhaps she was resigned to the thought that she wouldn't get any thanks from an ungrateful ex-pupil, so saw no point it signing the card.

However, I did write and thank her and I also sent her a piece of wedding cake. I hope it pleased her.

MISS SMITH

Maypole Dancing when I was May Queen, (second on the left) Miss Smith on the right

Miss Rose Smith was one of those ladies of whom it is impossible to tell their age, but I think she must have been in her late twenties or early thirties when I started school in 1940.

She, like Miss Leppard, was a deeply religious woman, but unlike our headmistress, who was a devout Anglican, Miss Smith and her family belonged to the Plymouth Brethren, a strict Calvinistic religion. Looking back I wonder how she managed to get a job teaching in a Church of England School, although she taught us Scripture in exactly the same way that Miss Leppard did and never talked about her personal religion.

However, we did learn that she wasn't allowed to dance, visit the cinema or do anything of a frivolous nature. This seemed terrible to me, because I loved music and dancing. Miss Smith didn't seem to miss any of those things. She was a serene and happy person, who smiled a lot. Her deprivations didn't seem to worry her at all.

She had two sisters, also teachers in Huntingdon schools, and they looked exactly like our Miss Smith! They all lived in Huntingdon with their parents, which meant that she had to cycle about three miles every day to get to school in Great Stukeley, but she was always there, no matter what the weather, come wind, snow, rain or hail. No one can remember her having a day off.

Miss Smith was of medium height with a solid, but quite slim figure. Her complexion, which had never seen a touch of make-up, was scrubbed clean and of a purplish hue. Her hair was pulled back into a loose sort of bun and fastened at the nape of her neck with a moiré ribbon in either dark green, navy or brown. She wore thick-lens, horn rimmed spectacles behind which her eyes looked crinkly when she smiled, which was often. In winter she wore hand knitted twin sets in sombre colours, thick tweed skirts and sturdy lace-up shoes and in summer she favoured demure box-pleated dresses in a discreetly patterned material, with Peter Pan collars and self belts. On her feet were plain leather Clarks sandals.

She was gentle and calm, the very opposite of our volatile headmistress, and an exceptionally good teacher. She was marvellous with the tiny children in her class in the Little Room and managed to teach them to read and write in a very short time, so that by the time they graduated to the Big Room at the age of eight, they had a good grounding in these skills.

She had very few materials to work with, but I am convinced that 3-8 year olds could not have had a better start to their education than they received at the Great Stukeley C of E School in Church End.

The Little Room offered some odd, and I suspect unique, activities and to this day I can't understand to what purpose they were performed.

The worst of these was something we called 'fraying' and we dreaded it! We were each given a piece of fabric about three inches square which we had to pull apart thread by thread, until we each had a little pile of shredded material on the desk in front of us. If we were given a loosely woven piece of fabric it pulled apart easily, but a piece of tightly woven cotton was so tough to fray that tiny fingers became sore and sticky, leaving the material grubby and damp. I can only assume that in those days of make do and mend, the piles of frayed material were used to stuff toys, although I never once saw the bag of threads that we produced used for anything. Whatever its purpose, this activity was used for years, because my sisters (four and a half years my junior) remember this most boring of pastimes and hated it as much as I did.

Much more exciting was when Miss Smith brought out the plasticine. This material had a curious smell and an all over sludge brown colour. No doubt it had been multicoloured at one time, but years of being mixed and moulded by countless grubby fingers had turned it into this singularly uninviting shade and given it its distinctive odour. No matter, we loved it and spent hours rolling it into long sausages, which we coiled round to make not very realistic looking snakes. We didn't have the skill or imagination to make anything really creative.

We were also given little individual blackboards to draw on. We were issued with a little piece of chalk and a damp rag for rubbing out. This was, I suppose, our 'free expression' time and we were allowed to draw whatever we wanted. The girls drew houses and the boys drew tanks, planes and other instruments of war. We weren't very original, I'm afraid!

Tuesday mornings was the time when Miss Smith put us through our paces. This was when we exercised our bodies as well as our minds, so out would come 'the equipment'. This consisted of a few bean bags, a skipping rope or two and some ancient hoops and sticks. The latter must have dated from when the school first opened. No child I knew ever played with a hoop and stick. It was exceedingly difficult to bowl these round on our steeply slanting playground, where the metal framed hoops would simply go off at an angle and fall over. Sedately throwing bean bags round in the presence of a teacher wasn't much fun either, but skipping was all right.

The activities were preceded by a few exercises of the 'bend, stretch, touch your toes' variety. If it was wet or too cold to go outside then we would do some indoor exercises like 'do this, do that' which was a version of 'Simon Says'. On very rare occasions we performed Country Dances to the accompaniment of a record played on an ancient wind up gramophone belonging to Miss Leppard. I presume Miss Smith's strict religious laws allowed her to instruct us, although she never actually took part herself. I loved dancing 'The Circassian Circle' and 'Strip The Willow' to the sounds of some scratchy recording.

One of my favourite things was when we played shops. We weren't allowed to do this very often for fear of the wear and tear on the equipment, which consisted of models of all kinds of goods that had been available before the war. There were dummies of cartons of cream, packets of jellies, blancmange and Bisto, tins of fruit and vegetables , soaps, toothpaste and best of all, great slabs of purple wrapped chocolate bars. I hoped against hope that one of these dummies might contain a bar of real chocolate!

Miss Smith would set up a counter while a couple of children would be shopkeepers for the day and the others would be the customers. We were given cardboard money in various denominations, (shillings, sixpences, florins, half a crowns, halfpennies and even farthings) and we then had to make our purchases, working out the cost and checking the change from the various 'shopkeepers'. Seeing all the pre-war goodies was an exciting

71

exercise for us children who hadn't seen large bars of chocolate or pots of cream for many a month. It also taught us to count. When the lesson was over the dummies were carefully packed away, the money counted and stored in the appropriate container and it was all stored away until we were allowed to play shops once more.

Miss Smith, like Miss Leppard, was very good at reading aloud to us. To the children in her class, whose imagination hadn't been blunted by television, it was like magic to hear the stories and see the characters come alive in our minds. It was in the Little Room that I was introduced to Rikki Tikki Tavi, The Jungle Book, the Brer Rabbit Stories, Winnie the Pooh and many others. Miss Smith would also read any suitable book we may have had for birthdays or Christmas and it was a great honour to have all the class listen to our own book.

Reading was a skill I longed to acquire. I loved stories and I desperately wanted to be able to read them myself, as there wasn't always a willing adult to oblige.

Miss Smith insisted that we write our names on everything we took to school and we carefully copied the unintelligible letters from her careful printing. Naturally, we learned our ABC which we recited phonetically as we drew the characters on our little black boards or onto sheets of paper.

I can recall so clearly the day I realised that I could read my own name and at once wrote it down, just to convince myself. This came about because my Wellington boots that I had worn to school that wet morning were standing by my desk. I had changed into plimsolls. Mum had written my full name inside the top rim of these boots so that they wouldn't get lost. All morning I had been looking at the words, when suddenly, as if by magic, I realised that they actually spelled out my name, MARGARET HARRIET WENDHOLT. I was so excited at this discovery, especially when I realised that I could also recognise other words as well, that I wanted to write them on everything … and probably did!

From then on there was no stopping me and I tried to read everything I could, easily recognising simple words and struggling over longer ones, where I needed an adult to help. I read newspaper headlines, labels on bottles, jars, packets and post-ers. Alas, I found it impossible to read without saying the words out loud and I'm sure I drove my parents to distraction with the monotonous intoning of a five year old trying to make sense of the written word.

Miss Smith also taught us simple arithmetic. We all knew our 'times table' before we left the little room and were proficient enough to do our 'add up, multiply, divide and take away sums' to please Miss Leppard, who went on to teach us the mysteries of fractions and decimals.

Miss Smith, who as Miss Leppard often told us, was not as qualified as our head teacher, so she occasionally had to go away on courses, and was soon able to boast 'letters after her name' though and when Miss Leppard was forced into retire-ment, she took over as head. With the help of a few itinerant teachers she managed to keep the school going until it finally closed sometime in the early fifties.

When children were eleven, Miss Leppard would try and coach them with the hopes of passing their Eleven Plus Exami-nation. This was not very successful and I can remember only two girls passing to go to the Grammar School. One was my friend Gillian Curtis, the other was Elizabeth Haynes.

I was very apprehensive about the Eleven Plus and in truth, didn't want to pass. I had heard horrendous tales of the cruelties performed on new kids at the Grammar School and the idea scared me. I had also heard Mum and Dad discussing how diffi-cult it would have been to provide not only uniforms, but sports equipment and other bits and pieces. It worried me that they couldn't afford it.

Children who didn't pass, were to go to a new sort of school that had just been set up. My friend Iris Turton and I were the first children from Great Stukeley C of E School to attend the Huntingdon Secondary Modern School, which was the old Coun-cil School situated at Brookside in Huntingdon. Here no uniform was required and the only thing that made it different from the Grammar School (as far as I was concerned) was the lack of a Sixth Form and therefore no chance to go onto university. Since hardly anyone I knew (apart from the 'gentry' in the village) ever went to university anyway, this wasn't exactly a worry for me.

Our preparation for the Eleven Plus was negligible. We were given some old papers to prepare us for the sort of questions we might be asked, but it was all Double Dutch to me. Some of the stuff we were asked was impossible for us to understand. My mind went blank and I didn't really try, because I had no idea what was required of me. Iris was the same, but neither of us felt ashamed at not passing. In fact, I was relieved and I am sure Iris was as well.

I can't remember feeling sad at leaving the village school, because when we broke up for the summer holidays we hadn't known for sure when we would have to go to Huntingdon. We had thought it would be September, but then it could have been Christmas. However, Miss Smith cycled up to see me in the school holidays to inform me that we were to report to the Secondary Modern School at the beginning of the autumn turn. So we left our little village school and our friends there without ceremony.

Going to the Big School in Huntingdon was a little worrying after spending seven years in our tiny village school, but it helped that Iris and I were to be 'new girls' together, so we could support each other.

We cycled to school together and although, (because she was a year older than me), we weren't in the same class, we did meet up at playtime and compare notes. Soon we had both made new friends, enjoyed the lessons and liked the teachers, so it wasn't long before we were both very happy and settled.

I was surprised and delighted to find that I wasn't as stupid as I thought (especially after failing to pass the Eleven Plus) and I was put into an 'A' stream and remained so for all my time at the Secondary Modern. I was never lower than second or third in the class and was often top. I think both Miss Leppard and Miss Smith can take some credit for this. Even though they had little equipment and an antiquated classroom in which to teach us, they did instil in me a desire to learn and an infinite curiosity about people, places and things. I was encouraged to write stories (compositions, as they called them) and was allowed to illustrate them. They answered all my questions as best they could and although I was appallingly bad at arithmetic, they still managed to get the basics into my head. That they did this whilst trying to educate children of vastly different ages and abilities is a miracle.

Both Miss Smith and Miss Leppard loved poetry, so we were encouraged to learn the classic poems by heart and became very competitive in trying to commit one to memory before anyone else. To this day I can still recite many of these poems. This is not unusual, of course. My mother could quote reams of Shakespeare when she was well into her eighties.

I don't know where Miss Smith went when the school closed down, but I assume she went on to teach elsewhere. She taught my sisters who are four and half years my junior, and after Miss Leppard retired she kept on all the old traditions. I went back just once to see my sister Irene crowned Queen of the May. By then I had left school and was working for my living. I know I couldn't help thinking how small the little classroom looked after going to the Secondary Modern.

The Great Stukeley Church of England School has long since been pulled down, houses built on the site and all village children are now bussed to other schools, but no matter how ideas on education change, or how sophisticated teaching methods become, I am convinced that no school children could have had a better start or been taught by a more dedicated teacher than our Miss Smith.

THE SCHOOL

Kathleen Deller (May Queen) with me on the right

The school stood at the bottom of Church End, about a couple of hundred yards from St. Bartholomew's Church. It was a brick built Victorian building of a design seen frequently throughout the British Isles. It stood high above the lane and had a steeply sloping tarred and gravelled playground that swept down from the main building to three steep stone steps by which access from the lane was attained. Flanking these steps was a lavender hedge that filled the air with perfume and bees on warm summer days. We children would gather the stems of flowers, which we would sell to our parents for a penny for a hundred. The rest was dried and rubbed, then used to make lavender bags during our needlework lesson, to give to our mothers, grandmothers, or aunts for Christmas … embroidered with their initials, of course!

The tarred and gravelled playground was quite steep and to the left had a fence to mark its boundary. Beyond this was an area of land that had been turned into allotments for the men of the village to Dig For Victory as the propaganda posters bade them do. To the right was a flower garden, tended by Miss Leppard, the caretaker and some of the children. It was bright with cottage garden flowers, like delphiniums, lupins, poppies and hollyhocks in summer, with a border of rampant pinks, whose heady perfume scented the warm days of early summer. Because this border was so thick and tangled, Miss Leppard would bribe a willing child with a penny to weed it during playtime or after school. My friend Iris and I often volunteered for this job.

There were two school buildings, the Big Room, which was the main part of the school and to the right, a narrow path led to the Little Room which was a long low building, which I think might have been part of a chapel. It had a front door, which was never opened, adjacent to the lavender hedge. It had a small overgrown garden with three steep steps leading up to the door. We always entered the Little Room by its side door, which was within the school grounds.

The Little Room was where Miss Smith taught all children up to the age of eight. Its title was not because of its size, but because it was the little children who occupied it.

It was a plain square room with an array of small desks and

chairs and a table and chair at the front where Miss Smith sat. Because the whole school probably only had only 30-35 children, there was room for storage and this was where the 'equipment' was kept. The hoops, ropes and bean bags for PT lessons, the goodies for our Shop game, the books, powdered ink, dipper pens and nibs etc. were all stored in boxes stacked to the side of the classroom area. It gave the room an untidy look, but we didn't care and neither did Miss Smith.

The main building, or Big Room, was completely separate from the Little Room and this was Miss Leppard's domain. It was quite large with a porch at either end. We entered by the door to the right and hung our coats on the pegs in the porch. The porch to the left was where Miss Leppard entered and this was forbidden ground to the children, as it was for her exclusive use.

The door from the porch to the schoolroom was large, heavy and arched, like a church door, with a fancy latch to open it.

The boarded floor was knotted, uneven and had no covering of any sort, so was worn and shabby from the feet of many children over the years.

The walls were plain white washed with high windows along one side, which had to be opened by a long pole. They were so high it was impossible to see out of them, so no outside views could distract us from our studies. All we could see were tantalising glimpses of blue sky on sunny days, or scudding clouds if it was wet.

Half way down the room to the left was a big slow combustion stove, surrounded by a tall guard, on which damp clothes could be hung to dry on wet days. This was the only form of heating, so we would gather round at break time to drink our free third of a pint of milk on chilly winter mornings.

When I first started school in 1940, we didn't have milk at break time. Every morning a couple of the 'big boys' would mix malted milk powder (like Horlicks) with water that was heated in a big kettle on the stove. It was served in little china mugs decorated with nursery rhyme characters. The lads who served it weren't too fussy or very expert at this chore and the resulting drink was lumpy and didn't taste all that good, but it was no doubt quite nutritious. Some years later little third of a pint bottles of milk were given to us. The milkman delivered it to the school in the mornings and left outside until required, because, of course, we had no fridge to store it. On cold days in winter, there was often an inch of frozen milk pushing off the caps, so they perched on the top of this frozen cream (no homogenised milk then). We tried to imagine that it was ice cream, but it tasted nothing like it. In summer we would have to force down the tepid greasy milk that was on the point of turning sour. It was disgusting, but we still had to drink it.

Miss Leppard's desk stood at the far end of the room. This was a most impressive piece of furniture and far grander than Miss Smith's. It was tall with a heavy lid which, when lifted, revealed all manner of interesting things. In here was kept The Register, The Punishment Book, pens, pencils, a bottle of red and a bottle of black ink, a round ebony ruler and some wonderful stuff in a little bottle that could be used to erase mistakes written in ink. It fascinated me to see Miss Leppard apply a little of this magical liquid to an error by means of a little glass rod, blot it with blotting paper and Hey Presto! the paper was clear of errors. I decided there and then to be a teacher when I grew up, so I could use this marvellous stuff whenever I made a mistake in my writing (which at the time was often!). I wonder what Miss Leppard would have thought of the wonderful Tippex that became my best friend when I first learned to type!

Behind this desk was her chair, which had to be as tall as the desk, so it had a little step so that she could climb into the seat.

When a child had a birthday, he or she was invited to stand on the step of this chair while the whole school sang 'Birthday Honours' to them.

This was not the usual Happy Birthday To You song, but a little ditty that was, I am sure, unique to our school.

This is how it went:
We wish you many happy returns of the day,
We hope you're very healthy and strong all the way.
Swift to do right,
Slow to do wrong,
And thoughtful to others all the day long.
After the birthday child had been serenaded with this song,

Miss Leppard would hold up each card the child had brought to school to show everyone, then she would read all the verses and messages. She would then give them a penny (from her own pocket, as she often told us). All this made us feel like a celebrity for the day, so birthdays were looked forward to and enjoyed, even though there were no elaborate presents as there are for children today.

Opposite the stove was the upright piano which was Miss Leppard's pride and joy. Upon this she accompanied our hymn singing and our renditions of folk songs she would have us sing for our Music Lessons. Before we were allowed to sing a jolly song like 'Little Brown Jug' or a melodious one like Green-sleeves', she would have us 'warm up our voices' with a lot of 'la, la, las', or 'coo, coo, coos' ending with a few 'ah, ah, ahs'. She seemed to enjoy this, but we felt self conscious and embarrassed, usually ending up in fits of giggles, which we desperately tried to hide from our teacher. This wasn't too difficult, as she sat at the piano with her back to us.

The piano was kept in tune by Mr. Dew from Huntingdon, who was a short, dapper man with crinkly hair and a ready smile. He used to come along just before May Day and work his magic, so the instrument was in good nick for the entertainment highlight of the school year.

We enjoyed his visits as a break from routine. Although the tuneless noises he made while tuning could be rather monotonous, he always ended a session with an arpeggio or two, then broke into a selection of jolly show tunes.

Miss Leppard once asked him to suggest a suitable song for us to sing at the May Day celebrations, in order to enlarge our repertoire. He suggested 'We'll Gather Lilacs' from the new musical 'Perchance To Dream', which was popular at the time. Miss Leppard approved of the song and thought it appropriate for the occasion and the time of year and we learned it in time for our performance. Another year he suggested 'Spread A Little Happiness', so we also sang that. It brought back many memories when the pop star Sting had a hit with it a few years ago! These modern songs were a nice addition to our more traditional repertoire.

On the wall to the right of the piano hung the famous picture 'When Did You Last See Your Father?' It depicts a small Royalist boy being interrogated by a Round Head Officer. If memory serves me right, it was a black and white print, as was the picture to the left, entitled 'The Vigil'. This showed a young girl in armour, kneeling before an altar, with a sword clasped in her hand and her eyes gazing piously aloft. She is bathed in a pool of heavenly light. I feel sure this was supposed to be Joan of Arc. There was one other large picture, in colour, called 'The Boyhood of Raleigh' (or was it Drake?), which showed the young explorer, listening to tales of an old seaman. This was, I am almost sure, by the artist Millais. Next to this hung a small print, which I suspect may have been from a picture by Gainsborough. It showed a pretty child in a green velvet suit and was called Boy With Rabbit. He held a white rabbit in his arms. We had a tea caddy at home with the same picture on it, so I assume that it must have been very popular at the time.

The only other wall decorations were a few sinister posters warning us of the dangers of Anti-Personnel bombs. We had to study these and make sure we didn't pick up anything that might be dangerous. I remember there was a rather pretty coloured one called a Butterfly Bomb. I don't think anyone ever saw one of these devices, but many, seeing an old tin can in a ditch, THOUGHT they did and got that delicious thrill of fear children love. Other posters told us 'Careless Talk Costs Lives'; 'Walls Have Ears'; we were urged not to be 'Squander Bugs' by a little cartoon character and told we must 'Make Do And Mend'. In fact, we were given endless advice on how to be a good, loyal and patriotic citizen... as if we had any choice!

I think it must have been after the war England had a plague of Colorado Beetles that decimated the potato crop. We had a poster on the school wall showing us how to identify this pest, a quite distinctive yellow and black insect. We were told if we ever saw one we must tell our parents as soon as possible, because it was a pest that was notifiable by law. One day my sister Marion, who was about six at the time, proudly presented my mother with a rather sorry looking ladybird and triumphantly announced, "Look, Mum, I found one of those cod liver oil beetles!"

83

At the end of the room by which we entered was a large china flower pot suspended from the ceiling on three sturdy chains. This pot was the home of an ancient Mother of Thousands plant. It was very vigorous with lots of little plantlets hanging from it. It was at its most prolific around the time we were rehearsing for our May Day celebrations and it was great sport to try and detach one of these plantlets as we held our ribbons aloft as we danced round the maypole. Sometimes a mistimed swipe would set the pot swinging wildly on its chains, much to our amusement and Miss Leppard's dismay!

Beside the porch where we entered the school was a strip of land that had been turned into a vegetable garden and here the boys were taught the rudiments of gardening. I seem to remember it was quite successful. The crops were always healthy looking and the produce was probably sold to our parents to raise funds for outings to Wicksteed Park or the seaside (after the war). We all had to help with keeping down the caterpillars that munched happily on the cabbages and were given jars of salt water and sent to pick them off and drop them in to their deaths, a messy and smelly business, but essential in those days before insecticides were available.

Right around the back of the school to the right of the building were the boys lavatories. The girls was round to the left. These were of the earth closet type, as were just about everyone's in the village. The farmers, landowners, professional people and the gentry had water closets and septic tanks, but not us ordinary folk.

I can't describe what the boy's lavatories were like, because they were strictly out of bounds to girls and vice versa. The girl's had two housed at right angles to each other and in separate buildings. The large one was for the big girls and therefore had a bigger hole to sit on, the little girls was lower, so tiny girls could reach and had a much smaller hole to sit on. It was a wooden boxed in affair, with a detachable front. Under the hole we sat on was a bucket, which when full the caretaker emptied into a large hole dug as far away from the school as possible. This hole was covered with a piece of corrugated iron. The caretaker poured a white powder over the contents. This was lime I think. When the hole was full, it was covered with a layer of soil and buried. It was quite smelly in summer, but was far enough away from the school building not to be too obnoxious.

After the war a special vehicle would come round the village once a week to empty our earth closets. This was know as 'the lavender cart'. Before that every resident had to empty and bury the contents themselves. It seems unhealthy and very primitive in this day and age, but everyone was in the same boat and we thought nothing of it. We were luckier than some, because ours was attached to the house, even though it was still outside. Many people had privies quite distance from the house, which wasn't much fun on a cold wet or snowy night.

During the war paper was in very short supply, so Miss Leppard took it upon herself to ration the toilet paper. She kept it locked in her desk, so if anyone wanted to go to the lavatory, they had to hold up their hand and ask permission to 'be excused', adding, "and please may I have some paper, Miss." The child would then approach her, whereupon she would solemnly tear off just two sheets of crisp paper from the roll in her desk, and present it to the child, who would then have to walk out of the room with as much dignity as they could muster, accompanied, no doubt, by a certain amount of sniggering from some of the children. The two sheet ration was hardly adequate and we found the whole procedure rather embarrassing, so after a while the system was changed. This may have been due to a parent complaining about the humiliation of their child having to ask publicly for toilet paper. However, the new system wasn't a lot better. The toilet roll was hung on a piece of string just inside the classroom door. There was no need to ask for paper, we simply helped our self to what we needed as we passed by the roll, but Miss Leppard still kept an eagle eye on us, making sure we didn't take too much. If we did, or made too many trips like this, then questions would be asked about our health! This could still be embarrassing, because the rustling and the ripping sound of a child tearing off paper was deafening in that quiet little schoolroom and the more careful one tried to be, the noisier it sounded. The best way was to just stroll by nonchalantly, rip off a few sheets and beat a hasty retreat. Children today (or their parents) would not allow such liberties to be taken with so personal a ritual, but then we accepted it as perfectly normal.

At home, during this paper shortage we used to use newspaper, which if Dad had time, was cut into squares and threaded onto a string, which was fine and gave us something to read whilst closeted in the privy, although this could be very frustrating if one became engrossed in a story, only to find most of it was missing!

I am sure we were exposed to many nasty germs because of these primitive toilet arrangements, but my theory is that we built up an immunity to them. There weren't the cases of food poisoning or 'tummy bugs' that there are today. We all survived to tell the tale anyway!

The only other furniture in the schoolroom were the desks and chairs used by the children. These had lids that lifted to reveal a space for the storage of books, paper, pens and pencils. Each desk had a small round hole at the back to accommodate a ceramic ink well. The ink powder was mixed with water in a large enamel jug, and the Ink Monitor poured the resulting liquid into the little inkpots. This was a messy job, the children often ending up with black smudges on faces, fingers and clothes. This ink had a strange smell and it often 'clotted', making it stick to the nibs of our dipper pens, blotting and smudging the paper as we tried in vain to copy Miss Leppard's beautiful handwriting. Heavy handed children often caused the nibs to become crossed, but the pens had to be in dire straits before Miss Leppard would let us have a new one. "Don't you know there's a war on?" She would say.

Along a couple of the walls were the cupboards that contained our supplies. Text books, exercise books, reams of paper (treated like gold dust!), pens, pencils and boxes of nibs, as well as the awful ink powder.

This is where I spent the first seven years of my school life. It was primitive grubby, with little or no modern equipment, but had two dedicated, God fearing women teaching us reading, writing, simple arithmetic, knitting, sewing, gardening, musical appreciation, English and even a little English Literature with of course, the all important Scripture, heading the list.

When I hear modern day teachers complain about the lack of resources, I think of Miss Leppard and Miss Smith and that little schoolroom in Great Stukeley and think that we were very lucky indeed. I will always remember them with affection and hope this account will be a fitting epitaph to them and those bygone days.

There is one little footnote that I would like to add to this chapter.

In 1955 when my husband Les and I were planning our marriage in St. Bartholomew's Church, we decided on 19th March for the wedding. We wanted to have our reception in the W.I. Hall, but found my childhood friend, Jean Cox and her fiancé, George Stillwell, had booked their marriage on the same day. So we weren't surprised to find that they had also booked the Women's Institute Hall for their reception (as was the custom in those days), so we had to find an alternative venue. The only place available in the village was the Schoolroom, so that is where we entertained our wedding guests. Not a very glamorous place, but it answered the purpose and everyone enjoyed themselves.

That was the last time I ever entered the building. Not long after that the school was pulled down and houses built on the site. No doubt the ghosts of the children who spent all of their schooldays there, still sit obediently and try to form perfect letters with cross nibbed pens, as Miss Leppard looks on.

THE VILLAGE
AND SOME
OF ITS
CHARACTERS

GREEN END

Great Stukeley was not a pretty, chocolate box kind of village, but during the 1940s and early 50s, it was just three lanes, Green End, Owls End and Church End, with a smattering of dwellings in between.

Green End was the first of these lanes as the village was approached from Huntingdon and it was here that, amongst the collection of farm cottages and other more modest houses , Mr. & Mrs. Thackeray lived in one of the bigger houses, complete with a beautiful garden. The Thackerays were very prominent citizens in the village, because Mr. Thackeray was the owner of one of the biggest building firms in Huntingdon. They also offered a funeral service. They had the reputation of employing high quality craftsmen and many of their carpenters and masons were employed to do restoration work to churches in the area.

Mrs. Thackeray was a stalwart of the Women's Institute as was Mrs. Juggins, wife of a farmer, who also lived in Green End. These two worthy ladies could often be seen bustling around the village, clad in tweeds, brogues and head scarves, as they went about their business. Miss Leppard was in awe of them, always asked them to school functions and treated them as V.I.P.s. I knew little about Mr. Juggins, except for the fact that he owned not one, but two Daimler cars. One for best and one for carting around sheep and other farm stock and implements. I think they had two children, Roger, also a farmer and Monica. I only knew these people by sight. I am sure I never had a conversation with either of them.

There were various other dwellings and cottages in Green End, some in terraces, some semi-detached and one or two stood alone.

One of the latter was the dark and forbidding Holly House, whose narrow front garden was filled with the holly bushes that gave it its name, along with some sinister looking yews, that must have blocked out a lot of light as they crowded the windows. This was the home of Sophie Fogel, a gruff voiced lady with a strange accent. We children were convinced that she was a witch, because she was quite ugly and seemed unfriendly to children. When I was older, I realised that Miss Fogel was a jolly

Yorkshire woman (hence the strange accent). She was a spinster and unused to children and probably had no idea how to speak to us, so with the wisdom of children, we were sure she didn't like us and must be a witch.

Also in Green End were the goats that Mrs. Haywood tethered to stakes by the roadside, in order for them to graze the grass verges. I was terrified of these animals with their vicious looking horns and weird slitty yellow eyes. I felt sure that they would butt me. They had an unnerving way of walking towards anyone walking in the lane. It was simply curiosity, I think, but at the time I thought they had different motives!

Mrs. Haywood was a gentle soft spoken Irish lady, with white hair. She had several evacuee children living with her and her husband over the years and a son, Basil, who lived in the village all his life.

In a terrace of cottages lived the Lovell Family, Arthur and Verina and their son John, who was a little older than me. They had an evacuee boy, George Stillwell, living with them, who was eventually to settle permanently in Great Stukeley and marry my friend Jean Cox. They brought up their four children and still live there today.

Next door were the Clarke's. Mrs. Clarke was a round lady, with a pleasant smiling face, I can't really remember what her husband looked like, but her youngest daughter Brenda, who was a little older than me, was a very pretty blonde haired girl, with a slim figure and happy disposition. She had an older brother Arthur and a sister, Olive, who was married to Harry Chance and lived elsewhere in the village, although it may have been in one of the other cottages in the terrace, although I can't be sure.

Other people living in Green End were Mr. & Mrs. Hobbs, their sons Russell and Roy, plus two other lads, Albert and Ronald Jacobs, who were orphans, I think. Ronald pumped the church organ for all services for many years. He eventually married Mary, a girl from Huntingdon and lived in a caravan in the field next to the Cox's thatched cottage in Owls End.

The other Mr. & Mrs Cox (no relation to my friend Jean) and their three daughters, Alice, Lily and Angela, lived in a semi-detached house by the Juggin's farm. Their next door neighbours were Mr. & Mrs. Sewell and their teenaged sons Douglas and Brian, there may have been a daughter, but I can't really be sure.

Where the lane ended there was a cattle grid and a narrow track led to Grange Farm, where lived George Gifford, one of three farming brothers in the area, the others being Tommy (who lived in Little Stukeley and was the father of Josh and Maser, the horse racing brothers) and Fred. They were all tall and dark with bushy eyebrows. George was a bachelor and was looked after by his housekeeper and cousin Miss Jessie Cooper, who was middle aged, tall and slim, with grey hair tied back in a bun. My friend Jean's father was cowman for George, so she and I would often visit the farm, though not by way of Green End, but across the fields from our lane, Owls End.

At the beginning of Green End by the main road, which was Ermine Street, stood a barn that was always referred to as The Blacksmith's Shop and indeed that was the official name for the bus stop there, but as far as I can tell, no one in the village could ever remember a blacksmith plying his trade there, although my friend Gill's mother said her Grandmother used to talk about watching a blacksmith at work. The building is there to this day and is still known as the Blacksmith's Shop.

Opposite this building was a large house that stood back from the road and here lived a well-to-do couple, Mr. & Mrs. Mole-caster. She was often seen in the village, clad in sheepskin jacket, patterned stockings, head scarf and sensible shoes, walking her collection of Border Terriers. The house was later the home of John Major, the MP for Huntingdon, who became Prime Minister, but I still think of it as 'The Molecaster's'.

A little way down the hill towards the village and along a little path was a row of cottages. In one of them lived Mr. & Mrs. Moon. I think they were Scottish. She was a quiet spoken lady, with pale gingery hair, who dressed in camel coats, colourful scarves and with a beret on her head. Mr. Moon was well known, for he was short, round with a rosy face, bald head and round glasses. I always thought that Moon was the perfect name for such a round man! He had extremely short, bandy legs and he used to ride around the village on a tricycle, that had big blocks on the pedals to ensure he could reach them. He was a very jolly looking man and he and his wife were well liked by the villagers. I think I am right in saying that their neighbours were Mr. & Mrs. Hitchcock, Mr. &. Mrs. Prior and their daughter Vivian and The Hamilton family.

At the bottom of the hill was a little lane leading off to the left . This was called Waterloo, it didn't have any houses and led eventually to Brampton Race Course and on race days, many villagers made the journey to watch from the road, or get in free after so many races had been run. I have made that journey myself many times, though not really caring for racing, I never ventured into the Race Course.

On the other side of the main road was The Lodge, which was at the front entrance (never used in my day) to Great Stukeley Hall, which was the home of the Fenwick family. In the Lodge, lived widow, Mrs. Deller and her five daughters, Alice, Rose, Betty, Ruby and Kathleen. There were many Dellers living in the village and it was always said that one should never speak ill of a Deller to anyone, because they were either a Deller themselves or married to one. No one would ever have spoken ill of Mrs. Deller of the Lodge, or her girls, because they were a very nice family. Kathleen, who was the best friend of Brenda Clarke, was a little older than me. She and Brenda were still at the school when I started there but left soon after.

The Lodge was in between two hills. At the top of the second one was the entrance to Owls End, to the right and the four Council Houses to the left.

The council houses were built in the 1930s , I would think, for they were pebble-dashed, as was the fashion in those days. In the first one lived Mr.& Mrs. Death, who were the grandparents of my good friend Gill Curtis. The other residents were Mr. & Mrs. Humphreys and their grown up sons, Mr. & Mrs Walsh with their schoolboy sons, Maurice and Peter. Peter was tall and thin and had a good head of wavy ginger hair and my sister Marion once referred to him as 'that boy with a heap of hair'. Which was an excellent description of him.

The last house in the row was occupied by Mr. & Mrs. Wally

Waldock and their family. Daughter Sylvia was a little younger than me, Brian was roughly the same age as my sisters and both attended the school. They had a baby brother, Trevor. Mr.Waldock's mother, known to one and all as Granny Waldock, also lived with them. She was round, short, with dark grey hair scraped back into a bun. She was a formidable lady and respected by all the children who had to pass by their house on their way to school, for heaven help any child who misbehaved in Granny Waldock's sight!

Beside their house ran the Cinder Path, which had a Kiss Gate at either end. This led to Church End , by way of a steep tarmac path to the right and straight on down another path to a little cluster of cottages called Moorfield, where my friend of many years, Iris Turton, and several other people lived. The cinder path was our short cut to school.

OWLS END

As I have already said, it was in Owls End I lived, at the time this was the least populated of the three lanes.

At the beginning of the lane, just a few yards away from the main road, stood the Women's Institute Hall, a green painted corrugated iron building, the hub of all the village entertainment. It was here we attended concerts, whist drives, dances, and various meetings. The cricket teas were served here and so were refreshments for the fete. Jumbles sales, bazaars, wedding receptions and twenty first birthday parties were also held there. It wasn't the most attractive building, but we loved it and enjoyed all it had to offer.

The Hall consisted of a long narrow room with a kitchen at the right hand end and the ladies cloakroom at the other. In the tiny cloakroom were rows of pegs for hanging coats and one toilet which had a rickety door separating it from the rest. The toilet was of course, the ubiquitous bucket type, but it was kept clean (and more or less odourless) by liberal doses of a white disinfectant powder, sprinkled in after use.

The gents didn't have an indoor toilet, but had to use a corrugated iron lean-to out near the bicycle sheds round the back. There was no car park, because no one except the farmers, the gentry and professional folk had cars. The cycle sheds were always full when there was an event on at the W.I. Hall.

The kitchen was home to an electric urn, several large brown enamel teapots, cups, saucers and plates, a sink (cold water only, I think) draining board and a table for preparing sandwiches and the like.

The main hall had chairs all around the walls and at one end was a stack of folding green baize card tables, erected for whist drives when required.

The floor was uneven and the knotted, unpolished boards had to have plenty of French chalk sprinkled on them to make dancing possible. There was a piano too, used to accompany the Women's Institute anthem 'Jerusalem' at their meetings, as well as other events that called for music.

The W. I. Hall was surrounded by an over-grown grassy area that wasn't really developed or cultivated, but simply cut in the summer to keep it tidy.

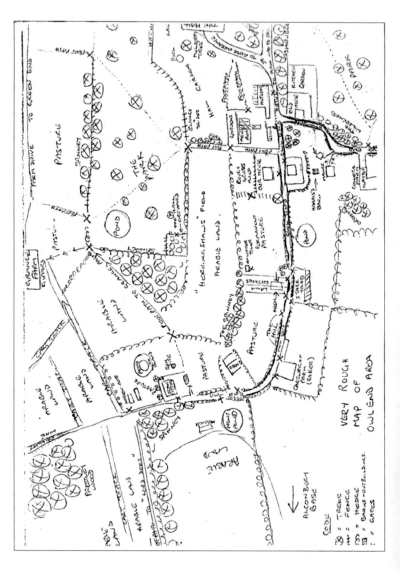

Very rough map of Owls end area

The next building in Owls End was College Farm, home to tenant farmer Mr. Clayton, his wife and two sons; Brian (who was my age) and Alan, a couple of years younger. I liked Brian and we often walked to school together. I loved to play in their orchard at the back of the farm house. They grew a great variety of dessert and cooking apples and we were allowed to pick up and eat as many windfalls as we liked. They kept pigs and I recall laughing at the antics of these creatures, let loose in the orchard, gorging themselves on rotten apples and pears, staggering about bumping into trees and each other, drunk on the fermenting fruit they had eaten. Of all the variety of apples there were in that orchard, the ones I remember best are those they called Codlings, a pale greeny yellow, with a shiny, greasy skin and a curious 'pleated' look to them. I think they were cooking apples, although they were probably eaten raw by us as well.

Mr. Clayton was a dark, quietly spoken man, with sharp features. He mostly wore a battered trilby hat for work, so I was surprised one day to discover that he had an abundance of very dark hair. His wife was a quiet spoken gentle woman, tallish, with light brown hair. She was always welcoming when I called at the farm. Years later, when I left school and went to work at a local pottery, Mrs. Clayton came there to work in the kiln room and was also a packer, so I got to know her as an adult and liked her just as much as I had as a child.

Brian was very like his mother, a stocky lad, placid and likeable. His little brother Alan had tight fair curls and was a sweet looking child of about three.

The Claytons moved to Huntingdon (probably after the war), where Mr. Clayton took a job in a factory. People were surprised to find he loved it and didn't miss life on the farm at all.

The farm was bought by the Porter family, Mr. & Mrs. Porter, their son, Ted and daughter in law Betty. I will be writing more about these people later. They became good friends of my family for many years.

Next door to College Farm stood the beautiful old Manor House, a big white painted building that stood back from the lane and approached by a wide drive flanked by an avenue of willow trees, which looked so delicate and pretty in the early spring sunshine. In truth, it was a misnomer to call it the Manor House, because it had never been that, but was an old granary that had been converted at sometime into the dwelling it was then.

This was the home of a rather eccentric family I will call simply Mr.& Mrs. P-S. Mr. P-S was much older than his wife and was a pale faced, stooped, grey haired man. His clothes always had a crumpled look to them and he wore a battered tweed hat on his head in winter and an equally battered sunhat in summer. He was a retired teacher. He walked with a pronounced limp, we were told was the result of a wound received in the Great War.

Mrs. P-S was of medium height, thin, with a head of frizzy, reddish hair screwed up into a chignon at the nape of her neck. Round owl-like glasses perched on the end of her nose. She wore a green suede suit most of the time and legend had it she had bought it for half a crown from a village jumble sale. She rode around the village on a sit-up-and-beg bicycle, inclining her head and smiling regally at everyone she met. Mrs. P-S had ideas above her station and once told my mother that in her young day children of the village had to curtsy and bow to 'the lady of the manor'. If she was advocating we did this, she had another think coming, for my mother told her in no uncertain terms, no child of hers was going to bow and scrape to anyone, let alone her!

The P-S family (they had a son, whom I shall call Robert, who was away at boarding school most of the time) were renowned for their eccentric diet. The two evacuee boys, David and Terry Allcock, who had the misfortune to be billeted with them, would bring along sandwiches for their packed lunch at school. It was always entertaining to see what the fillings were. Chickweed, rose petals and other strange weeds often featured. They would go home to Potato Peeling Soup, which was grey, greasy and unappetising to look at and even more disgusting to taste. Once, when I called in to see if they were ready to walk to school, I was amazed to see them sitting at the table with half a broken plate each, on which they had a whole raw carrot, covered with black treacle. This was their dessert.

The house always smelled of apples and I asked Terry and David why this was. They said it was because they stored all the fruit from their orchard in a room at the top of the house and often this would be rotten before it could be used, but this didn't stop Mrs. P-S making it into 'nourishing meals'. She once gave my mother a recipe for Rotten Plum Cake. We never tried it, I'm glad to say.

When I was walking home from school one day Mrs. P-S gave me a blue sugar bag full of apples so far gone they were causing the bag to disintegrate with the fermenting juice.

"Tell your mother that will be sixpence." She said.

I took them home and told Mum what she'd said. "You take them right back and tell her she can stick her rotten apples."

I was too scared to say that, so I simply climbed up the steep steps to her front door and left them there for her to find.

In the grounds of the Manor House stood a white painted bungalow and here lived Mrs. P-S's mother, Mrs. D-M and her daughter, whom I shall call Mildred (not her real name). Mildred was, as we used to put it then, a bit simple. She seldom spoke to anyone outside of her family, and when we saw her (never alone) she had a vacant smile on her face all the time. The only contribution Mildred (who was middle aged and looked a lot like her sister) made to village life was to make some very odd looking dolls that she presented to various functions for prizes or to sell.

Mrs. D-M was plump, with white hair piled high on her head and she always dressed in black ankle length clothes. She reminded me very much of pictures I had seen of Queen Victoria in a book my father used to read. She had the regal stance and haughty demeanour adopted by her younger daughter, Mrs. P-S.

Outside the Manor House was a very smelly ditch, causing a lot of complaints from neighbours in summer when it was hot. The contents of this ditch were grey and scummy and was, I suspect, an over flow from a septic tank. We used to approach that part of the lane, take a deep breath and run past as quickly as we could. It was like that for years and was very unpleasant indeed, and I am sure it was a health hazard, but nothing was ever done about it.

Opposite College Farm and The Manor House was a wooded area known to everyone as The Wilderness. This was part of the

Fenwick's Estate and was on the fringe of the parkland that belonged to Stukeley Hall. We would occasionally explore this little spinney, but it was really of no great interest to children. It didn't even have violets or primroses growing in it.

The next house in the lane was affectionately known as The Old House. This was the first building on the right of the lane, after the W.I. Hall .

No one lived in the Old House; it was to all intents and purposes a potting shed, where the gardener for the Stukeley Hall Estate raised plants for the market garden run as a commercial concern. They grew soft fruits, salad stuff and other vegetables in season and sold them to various greengrocers in Huntingdon and elsewhere. The gardener, whom I shall call Mr. Wood (not his real name) was in charge of this venture. He and his family lived in the house opposite ours.

Mr. Wood was of medium height, with a poker straight back, reddish purple face and bristling grey moustache. He wore a cloth cap, jacket with leather patches on the sleeves and a big canvas or leather apron for work. He looked and sounded like a Sergeant Major and had probably been a soldier in the First World War. His wife was a skinny, sour-face woman, with iron-grey hair cut into a severe bob. I can't ever remember this woman smiling. She was diabetic, so maybe she didn't feel well for much of the time and that was what made her so miserable. They had three daughters whom I shall call P, M and C. P was the eldest and had much the same demeanour as her mother. M was pleasant enough, as was C, who for a short time dated my Canadian cousin, Erwin. P was probably in her early twenties and the other two were teenagers. M was quite pretty and smiled often. She was friendly to our family and it was her husband- to-be who gave my sisters their first taste of bananas after the war. C was petite, with a dimpled smile and rather prominent teeth. We liked her and she seemed to like us.

Mr. & Mrs Wood hated my family with a vengeance for some reason and seemed to resent the fact we had come from London and were living in an estate house. They seemed to think we had no right to live there.

He was an Air Raid Warden, which meant he had to do the

rounds at night to make sure everyone's black-out was in place, with no chinks of light showing. He was very zealous in this pursuit and made my mother's life a misery by hammering on the door demanding that she "Put out that light!", even though her sole source of lighting was one paraffin lamp downstairs and a couple of candles up stairs. I doubt whether, even if there had been a chink in her blackout, the German pilots in their enemy planes would have seen her flickering lights and be guided to their targets! I think he just enjoyed bullying her, knowing she was a woman alone with a five year old and six month old twins trying to cope with living in an isolated village, after being in a city all her life. He and his wife seemed determined to make life as unpleasant as possible, not only for my mother, but we children as well.

Our house had a side gate reached by way of a path that ran from the lane to the Estate out buildings and beyond to the parkland and eventually to Grange Farm. This had a board at the entrance warning "Trespassers Will Be Prosecuted". We knew this didn't apply to us, because there was no other way we could reach the gate. However, Mr. Wood made it his business to inform us we weren't allowed to use it and we should use the front gate at all times. This became such an issue with him, my mother was forced to go to the Hall and see Old Mrs. Fenwick, the owner at the time, to get the matter cleared up once and for all. The old lady agreed that "Wood is being ridiculous, my dear, of course you can use the path to get to your gate." She added, with meaning, "I'll have a word with him." Round one to Mum!

He was even more annoyed when Mrs. Fenwick allowed Mum to use one of the empty out houses along that very same path to raise a few chickens, for eggs and possibly meat. This remained in use by my family until my parents moved to a new old people's bungalow in the village in 1976, but Mr. Wood was furious about it.

Gates seemed to be an obsession with the Woods. My sisters and I were swinging, quite gently, on the front gate one day, when Mrs. Wood came charging out and told us to stop it. "It's not your gate to swing on!" she yelled. "It belongs to Mrs. Fenwick and if you break it your parents will have to pay for the damage." Upset to be told off by someone we hardly knew, we went in and told Mum what she said. Off she went, rolling up her sleeves, to 'sort this matter out.' I don't know what was said, but it didn't improve matters between the two families.

Mrs. Wood was equally annoyed when Colin, an evacuee boy and I were floating sticks down the ditch that ran between our house and Lawn Cottages. She again charged out of her house and demanded we stop, because the ditch had been newly cleaned out and our sticks would block it. This was nonsense; we had one small stick each, the like of which could easily fall naturally into the water at any time. She was simply waiting for an excuse to nag us again. I don't think the ditch belonged to the Estate anyway.

I think the nastiest thing she did was when the Perry sisters (Joan, Iris and Joyce, evacuees who lived in the lane with various people) and I were walking along the aforesaid disputed path, where a large apple tree growing behind the wall of the Estate, had over-hanging branches. It was autumn and a lot of wind falls had fallen onto the path. We knew these would just rot away, as no one ever picked them up out of the abundance of nettles that grew there; so we sorted out the best, ate some and took some home. Mrs. Wood saw us and asked if we'd eaten any. We said we had. "Then you'll die!" she said, with a nasty grin. "They have been poisoned."

We were terrified and ran home to tell Mum we were all going to die.

She was furious and went round, yet again, to tell the mean-spirited woman a few home truths. Not that it seemed to bother her. I think she just enjoyed nagging children and probably liked the excuse to have yet another confrontation with my usually easy-going mother.

Why they hated us so much, I have no idea. They seemed to resent our very existence. We were not unusually naughty children. We never once cheeked them, or answered them back when they told us off for some imaginary misdemeanour. We would have been in trouble with Mum if we had, but they simply disliked us and lay in wait in order to find something they could moan about. Needless to say, we didn't like them either and to be honest, I was frightened of them.

To the left of our house was a dwelling where the Fenwick's Chauffeur had once lived, but now it was occupied by the Hutsons, a childless couple in their middle years. Mrs. Hutson was very short, very round and rather plain. She wore a camel coat in winter, with stout lace up shoes and a sort of pudding basin shaped hat of a similar camel colour to her coat. She huffed and puffed when she walked, due I suspect to her short stature and legs and stout figure. She was a regular church goer. Her husband, Dick, was a strange man, who spasmodically worked at Chivers the canning and jam factory in Huntingdon. He was epileptic and often unfit for work. They had a Pekinese dog called Suki, whom they both adored, but even our animal loving family couldn't take the snuffling, yapping little dog to our hearts.

Mum loved to recall the day Mrs. Hutson came running round to see her, begging for assistance. It seemed Suki was in season and a stray Alsatian had taken a shine to the little dog, who wasn't averse to the idea of a union, however it was proving a difficult job, because as Mrs. Hutson blurted out to Mum "Her poor little legs are right off the ground!"

Unfortunately, no offspring resulted from this 'marriage', but we did have great fun trying to picture what the puppies would have looked like!

A field away from us and on the same side of the lane were a pair of semi-detached houses, called Lawn Cottages. These were also Estate houses, the people living in them didn't work for the Fenwicks, except on a casual basis, but were, like us, tenants .

In the first lived Mrs. Barton and her son Donald, the bad boy of the school. Mrs. Barton was short, stocky and dark haired. She wore a navy blue belted trench coat in wet weather, with a purple beret worn at a jaunty angle and Wellington boots. She was a keen gardener and also loved doing intricate embroidery. Whenever I think of her house, I remember the gleaming front room, its highly polished furniture draped with numerous mats, chair back, arm rests, runners and table cloths, all beautifully embroidered in shades of mauve, purple, pink and blue, with occasional flashes of yellow.

Sometimes she would invite me to tea. Donald was so different then from the naughty child he was at school. We would sit quietly at the table colouring pictures with Donald's immaculate crayons. Then she would show me how to make the embroidery stitches. I was thrilled when I mastered the lazy daisy and was soon able to make a good job of satin stitch, stem stitch and French knots.

Mrs. Barton idolised Donald, who was her only child and when he was at home, he seemed to be angelic, but at school he was disruptive, violent, foul mouthed and a liar. Mrs. Barton never accepted he was naughty and blamed his lack of reading and writing skills on bad teaching, although Donald was the only child who was so badly behaved.

Because he lived next door (even though it was a field away) and he was only a little older than me, Mum would occasionally ask him to tea with us, but he wasn't always as angelic as he was at home and many times he had to be sent home for behaving badly.

Next door to the Bartons lived Mr. &. Mrs. Allen and their two teenage daughters, Nelly and Betty. Mr. Allen worked for the railways company delivering parcels in a strange looking little three wheeled lorry. He didn't keep this vehicle at home, but cycled into work every day to pick it up from the depot. He was a very steady driver and doubtful that he ever exceeded twenty miles an hour! He wore his navy blue uniform constantly, complete with bicycle clips and he even dug his garden whilst wearing them. In fact, his daughter Betty swore he would turn up to give her away on her wedding day in the uniform and cycle clips. I remember looking especially, but was disappointed to find he was in a smart suit, minus the clips!

He was short and balding, with a ring of ginger hair showing beneath his cap. He had a bristling ginger moustache and eyebrows to match. A taciturn man, I doubt I ever said more than "Hello" to him in all the time I knew him. His wife was short, very round and had the kind of voice that made one think she was unhappy all the time. She seldom smiled, but was really a very pleasant woman. She seemed to wear a permanently worried look on her face and the severe iron grey hair, cut into a short

'Eton crop' (I always thought that was 'eaten crop', because of the chewed off look to the style!) anchored with a large hair grip didn't help to soften her looks at all. Both she and Mr. Allen preferred to keep themselves to themselves. I don't think either of them ever entered our house during all the time we knew them, although their daughter Betty was a regular visitor of ours, and even Nelly had called from time to time.

The two girls were in their teens when we first knew them. Nelly was dark, serious, quiet and rather plain, with prominent teeth and the same sort of whining voice as her mother. Betty, on the other hand was a lively, bubbly girl, pretty, with light brown hair, worn in the fashionable style of the day. When she came to see us (which was often) the house was full of laughter and fun. Both girls biked into Huntingdon every day to work, Betty at the Hosiery Mill, which was in full production making socks and underwear for the forces and Nellie at the Huntingdon Model Laundry.

I loved it when Betty was around. She was funny, with a fund of stories to tell about her various boy friends that had everyone laughing. She had a string of American beaux, who were constantly beating a path to her door. She became engaged to one of them, but she eventually married John Price, a good looking young man from Little Stukeley. Nelly surprised everyone by marrying a G.I. called Dewey. He was from Indiana and had a slow Southern drawl. Nelly's marriage didn't last, but she had taken to life in the States and when she remarried and returned to England for a visit, she had acquired the same Southern drawl as Dewey and looked every inch the American matron.

The Allen sisters were like chalk and cheese, but both very nice girls in their own way.

A little further up the road and on the left was Cartwright Farm, the home of a youngish farmer, George Baker and his sister Janet, who kept house for him. I believe the Bakers also owned College Farm, but I can't be sure.

George was a quiet and rather withdrawn man, not exactly friendly, although Janet (or Miss Baker, as I called her) was a very nice lady. They had taken in a very exotic evacuee and her daughter. Pearl was Jewish, a large blowsy woman with a cock-

111

ney accent and a liking for gaudy coloured clothes and cheap jewellery. Her daughter Connie was about thirteen at the time and attended our school, though we thought it very strange she wasn't allowed to go to the church services or share in our Scripture lessons at school. Connie was beautiful, with lustrous black hair, olive skin and enormous dark eyes. Miss Baker once asked Mum and us girls to have tea with Pearl and Connie. I suppose she thought Pearl and Mum would get on well, as they were both Londoners, but Pearl was (as Mum put it) 'a bit of a gor' blimey' and Mum was a stickler for speaking properly. All they had in common was the place of their birth, but even that wasn't that significant; Pearl hailed from the East End and Mum was from North London, which might as well have been another country in those days.

Pearl's son Izzy would occasionally visit his mother and sister. He was very dark, with slicked back, Brylcreemed hair. He wore the sort of suit worn by what we called 'wide boys' or 'spivs'. These suits had wide legged trousers, draped jackets with wide lapels, topped with a wide brimmed hat, worn at a jaunty angle. Everyone suspected Izzy was active in the black marketing of goods. He didn't have a regular job, but always seemed to have plenty of money and expensive clothes.

Pearl hated life in the isolated village and soon she and Connie moved to Huntingdon, where they became very well known for reasons I won't go into here!

Next along the lane were two houses that had been farm cottages belonging to the Bakers. When we first moved to the village one was occupied Mr.& Mrs. Haynes and their sons Peter, (nicknamed Hector, for some reason) who was about fourteen and Harry, a few years younger. They eventually moved to another house in the village. Mr. Haynes was for many years the verger at the church.

May and Jup Lyons then moved into the house and it wasn't long before May gave birth to Richard. These people were to become great friends of my family for many years. I will be writing about them in other parts of this book.

For some reason I can't remember who was living in the other house adjoining theirs at first, but later on a variety of families lived there. The Manchetts and I think George Baker's sister-in-law and family lived there for a while, but I may be wrong.

The very last house in the lane before the gravelled road petered out into a cart track leading Presley Wood, was the thatched white cottage where my friend Jean Cox and her family lived. However, when we first moved into the village this cottage was occupied by Bill and Lizzie Cobley. We were told that these people were gypsies and it wasn't hard to believe. Lizzie was well into her seventies, wrinkled, with wiry, untidy grey hair. She always wore a slightly grubby wrap around overall and run down shoes. She smoked incessantly. Bill wore a peaked cap, worn at an angle, a red kerchief round his neck, corduroy trousers, a collarless shirt and a shabby jacket. He was often seen wending his way home from the Three Horseshoes, staggering along the lane, after a few ales.

When they moved to another part of the village, the Cox family moved into the cottage. Jean was to become my friend and we spent many hours together playing in and around her pretty home.

I will be writing more about my friendship with Jean and the good times we shared in and around her cottage later on in this book.

Those then were the people who inhabited my lane and were my neighbours way back then.

Back on Ermine Street just a little further up from the Council Houses stood a big detached residence that rejoiced in the name of Denmark House. Elderly Mr. Grice lived here. He was thin, white haired and stooped. He spoke with an educated accent and was obviously quite well to do. Later the house was occupied by a really nice couple, Mr. & Mrs Gilmour, who seemed very old to me, but they were probably in their early sixties. He always wore a Panama hat, cotton jacket and trousers in summer and was of medium build with grey hair. Mrs. Gilmour dressed in plain, but expensive looking clothes. Both were extremely friendly and joined in all the village activities. I remember once when my friends and I wanted to put on a firework display and communal bonfire one Guy Fawkes Night, the Gilmours allowed us to build the bonfire in their paddock at the rear of the house. Our mothers supplied refreshments and our dads lit the fireworks. It was an excellent evening and we made quite a substantial sum to donate to what was called 'The Bunny Fund'. The Bunny Club was run by the local paper, the 'Hunts Post'. It ran competitions and a birthday club (members got a birthday card from Uncle Bunny), but the main reason was to raise money to buy beds for the Children's Ward at the County Hospital, which it did very successfully. Our few pounds were sent on to them and we got a mention in the next week's Hunts Post. Heady success indeed!

The Cinder Path ran between Gilmour's Paddock (flanked by a tall hawthorn hedge) to the right and Waldock's garden to the left.

I seem to remember a couple of donkeys in the paddock.

A little way along Ermine Street was the low, attractive Sunnyside Cottage and here lived pretty little Mrs. Cade and her equally pretty little boy Raymond, who was about the same age as my twin sisters. He had light curly hair, blue eyes fringed with long dark lashes and a sweet smile, just like his mother. I think his father was in the forces at the time. They were a shy and reserved family. A little further along was the entrance to Church End. Opposite this on the other side of the road was the pub, The Three Horseshoes, which was a low thatched building painted a rich terracotta colour. The landlady and landlord were an elderly couple, Mr.& Mrs. Crow. She was tiny, thin and birdlike, with grey hair scraped back into a tight bun. He was stocky, with a bristling grey moustache, red nose and purplish complexion. He kept a few cows in a field adjoining the pub and cycled round the village balancing huge cans of milk on his handlebars, selling it to anyone who wanted fresh milk. Mum would go to the door with a jug and Mr. Crow would ladle out the amount she required. His big ladles measured either a pint, a half pint, a quarter pint or a gill. I don't suppose this milk was pasteurised and it certainly wasn't homogenised! But we drank it every day, until he retired and the deliveries ceased.

There must have been something that connected the sale of milk and beer. Mr. Harris, gingery haired and clad in equally gingery tweeds, was the landlord of The Bell at Little Stukeley and he also kept cows and sold milk. His herd was kept in Owls End in a field (always known as Harris's Field) adjacent to the Manor House.

I seldom had reason to enter The Three Horseshoes, except on the rare days when I earned a penny for organ pumping or weeding the pinks border at school; then I would go, probably with Gill or Iris and purchase an arrowroot biscuit. These were big round, dry and rather uninteresting biscuits, but like heaven to us! To purchase this we had to go round the back of the pub to the Tap Room, which had a stone floor and smelled (not un-naturally!) of beer. There were rows of glasses and jugs on shelves. If a customer wanted a glass of beer, Mrs. Crow would disappear down a flight of stone steps to the cellar, emerging a few minutes later with a jug of foaming ale, which she would transfer to the glass (pint or half pint). They sold mild, bitter and stout. I don't think they had a licence for spirits in those days, although I can't be sure because neither of my parents frequented the pub on a regular basis and I was never allowed to enter the saloon or public bars.

The Vicar called the Three Horseshoes, 'the little red house' and I was convinced that unspeakably evil things went on there because he always sounded disapproving when he spoke of it.

CHURCH END

The last lane in the village was Church End, the most populated lane of the three.

Right at the top, nearest the Main Road, on the right were a
couple of farm houses, now a rather nice restaurant. In one of
them lived a large family, who moved out soon after I started
school. The only reason I remember them at all was that one of
the sons of this large brood of children, Keith Bullock, was about
my age. We shared a birthday, which was a novelty to me, because I had never known anyone with the same birthday as me
before.

Next to them lived the Gilletts. Mr. Gillett was short and
stocky, with a red face and a good head of brown curly hair. He
worked for a local farmer and was a lay preacher at the chapel in
Little Stukeley. His wife was about the same height as him and
had a well rounded figure, a round rosy face and hair arranged in
tight curls. The round look was completed by a pair of round
spectacles. They had a young son called Raymond, a pixie-
faced little boy, with a freckles and sandy hair. He was about the
same age as the other Raymond (Cade). Mr. & Mrs. Gillett always sang in the village concerts, as I will be relating in another
chapter of this book.

Down the road a little and to the left was a row of two up two
down, cottages, Kitchener Terrace. I am not sure how many
houses were in the row, but it must have been about six, I think.

At No. 1 lived my friend Gillian Ruth Curtis with her mother,
Tilly and father, Ted. The houses were tiny with a communal
back yard, joined by a cobbled path. Outhouses stood a few
yards away from their back door. This is where the earth closet,
coal and general purpose shed stood. Beyond the outhouses
was a field where many a children's birthday party was held.
Along with just about every other child in the school, I have enjoyed the delights of jelly and blancmange, egg and cress sandwiches and birthday cake, served at a long trestle table covered
with a white sheet, in that field.

A couple of doors away from Gill's family lived Mr. & Mrs. Burton and their sons Laurence, a little younger than me and Derek,
a little younger than the twins. Mr. Burton was tallish and dark.
The thing I remember most about him was seeing him with his

ferrets, one of whom he called Maggie, which being the diminutive of my name, made it stick in my memory. Laurence was as dark as his father, a nice and very good looking lad, who eventually joined the navy. I remember how handsome he looked in his uniform! Derek was more like his mother, who was a pleasant, serene-looking lady, with a ready smile.

Miss Warne, the Vicar's housekeeper, also lived in Kitchener Terrace after the Vicar's death, alongside several elderly widows, whose names escape me. I can remember the name of only one, a jolly, fat lady with white hair. Everyone called her Old Mrs. Sly, to differentiate from her daughter-in- law, Mrs. Sly, the mother of Ian and Anita and wife of Denny, who earned a living as a press photographer in London. Mrs. Stukins was Mrs. Sly's sister, so Keith and Christine Stukins were cousins to Anita and Ian. Keith was a really nice lad, several years younger than me. Christine, a pretty little doll-faced child, was a few years younger than her brother. Bob Stukins, their father, worked for the post office for many years. Thinking about the people in the village, it puzzles me why we called the men by both their names, yet their wives were always referred to as Mrs. I knew that Mrs. Sly was called Mary and her sister was Eva, but even my parents called them Mrs., but their husbands were always referred to as Bob and Denny.

I can't remember who else lived in the Terrace, except for a Mrs. Townsend and her little daughter June. They were newcomers to the village, and were at one time joined by Mrs. Townsend's sister, Mrs. Preston. She was married to an American serviceman and had a baby son she called Jefferson Arthur Junior. The two sisters were dark and attractive and seemed quite young compared to the other mothers with children at school in the village. June was a pretty dark-haired little girl. She and Gill became good friends. The only thing I really remember about June is the time she was wheeling Junior along in his pram. He was crying, so she turned the pram round so the sun shone onto his face. "That will make him close his eyes and he'll go to sleep." she said. It worked, but I doubt his mother would have approved!

Down the road a little and to the right were three bungalows, more modern than most of the houses in the lane at the time. The Vicar lived in one with Arthur, his green parrot. Occasionally, Arthur would escape from the custody of his cage and take up residence on the roof, where he could be heard telling passing sparrows and blackbirds that "Arthur's a pretty boy!" The Vicar would try to coax him down and would sometimes try to dislodge him with a long stick, but he was a stubborn bird and refused to budge until he was good and ready. There was little chance of him flying away, because he was a wise old bird and knew only too well which side his sunflower seeds were buttered!

For a short while an Air Force Officer, his wife and young daughter, Jane, who was about my age, lived next door to the Vicar. Jane Curzon was a pretty, well spoken little girl. She and I were soon good friends, so much so that Mrs. Curzon, as pretty and nicely spoken as her daughter, asked me to tea with them. Mum took me there and fetched me at the appointed hour. She was concerned in case I should let her down with my table manners, but I had been schooled well by her and I am sure I did everything as I should. I know I said "Thank you for having me." as we were told to. I was asked to go again, so I'm sure I didn't do anything outrageous! The Curzons moved away soon after that and the Stratton family moved in.

The last occupants of the bungalows were Mr. & Mrs. Rollinson (or was it Rawlinson?) and their daughter Dorothea. Mr. Rollinson was a business man, always dressed smartly in suit and tie. He was enormously fat, with a red face and grey, thinning hair. He was also very tall. I think he must have been older than his petite and pretty wife. She had beautifully dressed wavy hair, wore rimless glasses and make up, which very few of the village women did, except maybe for a quick slick of lipstick on special occasions. I remember seeing her walking in the village with high heeled shoes on her incredibly tiny feet. Dorothea was a teenager who attended the Grammar School when I first knew her and she was very like her mother. Tiny, with a lot of pretty brown wavy hair. Dorothea served in the WRNS and looked very sweet in her uniform. When at the age of fifteen, I started work at The Fen Potteries in Huntingdon, Dorothea was employed there as a decorator, so we worked together as col-

121

leagues for a while. Her husband, Herby Wingrave, had served as a pilot in the RAF and looked every inch an airman with his handle bar moustache. After he was demobbed, he was a teacher at the Huntingdon Secondary Modern School and taught me geography. It seemed odd to me to be on first name terms with my teacher's wife in those more formal days. I liked Thea (as I then called her) and she seemed to enjoy working with me too.

After the bungalows and on the same side of the road was The Old Rectory, a big tumble down house with a huge and rambling garden. It was no doubt considered too big for the bachelor Vicar to live in, so for a lot of the time it was empty, although I do remember a friend of my mother's, Madge Haynes, living there with her husband, Herby and baby daughter Elizabeth, who was a surviving twin, the other baby girl died (I think) at birth. This was probably why Mum and Mrs. Haynes became friends, having both given birth to twins.

I remember visiting the family at the Old Rectory and loved exploring the garden, which was over grown and ideal for playing in. There was a paddock in front of the house, which was the home of several pear and walnut trees and a perfect place to 'scrump' the fruits from these trees (as I have related in another part of this book.)

A path led from the Old Rectory to the side gate of the church, by which Vicars of bygone days gained access.

The Church of St. Bartholomews is beautiful and was mentioned in the Doomsday Book Survey, although nothing of that church remains today. There are indications a stone church existed in the 12th Century, but most of the building was carried out in 14th and 15th Centuries, with restoration taking place in Victorian and Edwardian times. I was married there in 1955 and my husband had his funeral service there in July 2002. My sister Irene, who still lives in Great Stukeley, was also married in the church, her two daughters, Louise and Amanda were both christened and married there. My sister Marion, who has lived in California since 1969, wanted her two daughters to be christened in the church, because she wanted them to be in the parish records of Great Stukeley. Her eldest daughter JoAnne was christened before they left for America, but Sarah, her youngest, was baptised when they returned for a holiday in 1973. So although not regular churchgoers, this building has been very important in our lives.

Next door to the church was the pretty white painted and thatched Glebe Cottage, which was the post office. It was run by a formidable lady known to one and all as Nanny Bull, the mother of Mary Sly and Eva Stukins.

She was short and stout, with dark hair scraped back into a severe bun. She was very deaf, which made using the Post Office a bit of a trial, especially for children. There wasn't a door that opened to admit you to the Post Office, but just an ordinary front door that led into Nanny Bull's living room, so we had to hammer on the door until she heard us.

She would then fling open the door, demand to know what we wanted and be quick about it! I remember Mum once asking me to get her a 'tuppenny ha'penny' stamp. Nanny Bull told me she had sold out and to come back another day!

Mum was once annoyed when she went to get her family allowance, which she'd saved for a week or two in order to buy the twins new shoes. Nanny Bull said "Hard up this week, are you?"

A little down the lane and on the same side of the road as the church and opposite the school, was a brick house standing sideways to the road. When I first started school this was a little sweet shop run by an elderly lady, Mrs. Allsop. She was small and thin, with the usual scraped back hairstyle that ladies of a certain age seemed to adopt back then. Her face was waxy pale and she had no teeth. I only ever remember seeing her in a floral wrap around overall over her skirt and blouse. Mrs. Allsop's daughter Lily, a friend of my mother, lived with her. Lily's husband Bill was in the Air Force. They also had Lily's niece, Marian Tasker, living with them. She was about the twins age, a pretty little girl, who was the envy of all the other girls in the school, because she was always beautifully dressed (and utterly spoiled) by her adoring Aunt Lily.

I don't remember a counter in the shop. I think Mrs. Allsop simply had boxes of the kind of sweets schoolchildren liked which she doled out as we paid her our pennies. There were sherbet dabs, rolls of Spanish liquorice, bull's-eyes and humbugs and the huge and wonderfully magical gobstoppers that changed colour as they were sucked. The shop smelled delicious! The shop closed soon after I started school, so maybe the children's pennies weren't enough to make it profitable, or perhaps the worry of taking sweet coupons when they were rationed was too much of a headache. When it closed it was the last shop Great Stukeley had until the late sixties, when a general stores opened on the new housing estate that was built opposite the Lodge.

After Mrs. Allsop's house, Church End divided into two with the School House standing at the centre of the fork. Miss Leppard lived for many years in this building, which was probably contemporary with the school. It was quite a big house, solid and very Victorian looking, surrounded by a pretty cottage garden. Miss Leppard moved from there into a wooden bungalow a little way along the path that forked to the left. It was in this bungalow Miss Leppard ended her days, I think.

Behind the school's Little Room ran a narrow passage and here lived Mr. & Mrs. Maile and their pretty dark haired teenaged daughter Jean. I always thought it funny that after Nanny Bull retired from running the post office, the job was taken on by Mrs. Maile. A very appropriate name indeed!

The next house along opposite Miss Leppard's bungalow, was a moderate sized house where Mr. & Mrs Eaton and their French companion, Madamoiselle Lefarge lived. The Eaton's were very reserved, had no children and didn't join in any of the village entertainments. They were middle aged, middle class and smart, if a little old fashioned, in their dress. Mrs. Eaton wore high necked dresses in dark colours, as did Madamoiselle (which is what we all called her). Mr. Eaton wore stiff starched high collars, suits and always a hat. Thinking back now, he looked the epitome of Edwardian fashion. People found the relationship between these three people very intriguing. It was a strange 'ménage a trios' unheard of in those days. I am sure it was all very innocent, but I think our parents enjoyed the idea of a whiff of scandal connected to these somewhat remote people.

Madamoiselle spoke with such a thick French accent that it was difficult to understand her. When we passed her in the lane we would sing out "Good morning, Madamoiselle", to which she would reply and incline her head slightly with a shy little smile.

The cottage next door to the Eaton's was that of Mrs. Papworth, a lovely old lady. Grey haired and smiling. She always had a cheery word for the children and their mothers as we made our way past her house to school. Her garden always looked beautiful and was a picture in spring with its swathes of purple aubrietia, clumps of daffodils, tulips and violets. After her house the path rose steeply until it reached the kissing gate at the end of the Cinder Path.

The fork to the right of the School House led to an area called Moorfield where there were several cottages. I am afraid memory fails me as to who lived in these houses, except for the very last one, which is where my good friend of many years, Daisy Iris Linda Turton lived with her family. I seem to recall this was where Mr. & Mrs. Gough and their two sons John who was a teenager and George who was about my age, lived. They both attended the village school. I think I am right in saying the Gilbert family, with sons Dennis and Bernard, also lived in this area. Dennis was one of the lads who mixed and served the Horlicks for our school.

That is about all I can remember of the people living in the three lanes that is called Great Stukeley.

The village has changed and grown so much since those far off days. The Park, the beautiful land surrounding Stukeley Hall, has been built on and is now divided into Chestnut Grove, Elm Road and Birch Avenue, where up market homes house a new population of villagers. Every one of the original three lanes has new houses.

The first of these new estates were the council houses that were built just after the war. These were erected on the hill over looking Moorfield and given the name Moorfield Way at first, but the name has since been changed to West View. Iris and her family were one of the first to move into one of these brand new houses that boasted all mod cons … no more earth closets! My sister Irene and her husband David have lived in West View for many years, bringing up their young family and enjoying being a part of village life. They eventually bought their house, as did all

125

the other residents in this part of Great Stukeley. The name Moorfield Way now refers to the bungalows that have spread out over the land between Ermine Street and Church End. My parents lived at 18 Moorfield Way from 1976 until my Mother died in 1992. They were very happy there and enjoyed the wonderful community spirit that still exists in Great Stukeley.

I haven't lived there since 1957, but a part of my heart will always be in Great Stukeley.

MAY DAY

Gill Curtis (May Queen)
Circa 1948

To the twenty or thirty village children attending the school in the 1940s May Day was probably the highlight of the year.

This event was not celebrated on 1st May as is usually traditional, but on Ascension Day, which falls on the last Thursday in May. This was chosen in order to tie in the pagan festival with the religious celebration of Christ's crowning in Heaven.

Miss Leppard and Miss Smith worked very hard to put on this event and the children also did their bit to make it a success.

The pattern of the celebrations never varied. Each child was expected to perform in some way, by reciting a poem, singing a song (as a solo or duet with a friend), or playing an instrument. We had a fairly free choice of material, providing it was 'suitable'.

Miss Leppard's method of choosing the May Queen was very simple. It was always the oldest girl in the school, which meant that every girl had the opportunity before she left the school, but nobody could be May Queen twice. It was my turn in 1947, my friend Iris was crowned the year before and Gill the year after.

A few days before the celebrations, Miss Leppard would bring out a large wicker hamper that was stored in the Little Room. This contained a selection of dresses (all smelling strongly of moth balls) from which the girls could choose which they would like to wear for the great occasion.

Who made these dresses and when was a mystery to us, but they were all of the same basic style, round neck, elbow length sleeves with gathered ankle length skirts. They were made from a sort of crepe material in pastel shades of blue, green, yellow, pink and mauve. Some were plain and some were decorated round the neck and sleeves with ribbon or braid. In truth, they were spectacularly unflattering, but we thought they were marvellous. The year that Iris was May Queen I discovered in the depths of the hamper a deep rose pink dress of the same material and style, but covered with embroidered red and pink roses. Miss Leppard told me that it was the Rose Queen's dress. I'd never heard of the Rose Queen before, neither had any of the other children. I begged Miss Leppard to let me wear it, when, as Maid of Honour , I crowned my friend Iris Queen of the May. She allowed me the privilege and I thought I looked very glamorous indeed!

The May Queen's mother was expected to provide something a bit special for the occasion, usually a long white dress and a crown of some kind.

I was very envious when Iris was allowed to wear her sister Dorothy's white satin wedding dress. Gill wore a bridesmaid's dress when it was her turn. For my part, I was proudly arrayed in a white satin underslip that had been worn beneath Betty Allen's wedding dress and she also lent me a white blouse made of parachute silk, a material highly prized in those days. This blouse had wide sleeves with tight bands at the wrist and was tucked into waist of the slip. My Dad made me a crown of silver paper covered cardboard that had stars joining points all the way round it. Borrowed white sandals completed the picture. I have photographs of me in this ensemble and I think I looked pretty good! My normally, wild and untidy hair had been coaxed into curls by rags and setting lotion the night before, so I felt I looked my best.

After morning service at the church, a party of girls went with Miss Smith to the Park, where we had permission to pick boughs of flowering horse chestnut and hawthorn blossom. We returned via Miss Leppard's garden where we gathered lilac, laburnum and any other flowering shrubs that took our fancy, then we giggled our way excitedly back to school, where Miss Leppard was supervising the arrangement of the schoolroom for the afternoons entertainment.

Miss Leppard fastened a T-square to the back of her tall chair and we covered this with the blossoms we had picked, transforming it into a flowery throne for the May Queen to sit on in regal splendour.

Sprigs of hawthorn and laburnum were draped over "When Did You Last See You Father", "The Vigil" and "The Boyhood Of Drake", adding a breath of spring to the rather staid pictures. We placed jam jars of buttercups and cow parsley on the windowsills. The little school room smelled sweet with the scents of the flowers.

Rows of chairs were drawn up to accommodate the audience of mothers, grandmothers, aunts and little children. Pride of place (and the best chairs) were given to the School Governors, one of whom (Mr. P-S) always gave a speech. The year I was May Queen he inadvertently gave Mum a tip for the Derby! He had spoken of me and my name, explaining that it meant 'Pearl'. There was a horse running in the Derby called Pearl Diver, so Mum put a shilling each way on it and won!

The other VIPs were the farmers wives and Mrs. Thackeray. There were seldom any men present, for most were working or still in the Forces.

The performance began at 2pm and just before that Miss Leppard, resplendent on her gown and mortar board (the only occasion we ever saw her in it) would be twittering and fussing round the VIP ladies and the Vicar.

This gown was truly splendid, black with pearl grey lapels of corded silk. One never to be forgotten May Day, Donald Barton decided to be on his very worst behaviour. Just before the guests arrived a tussle with Miss Leppard followed during which he flung an ink pot, filled with the disgusting black powdered ink, at the teacher and a huge black stain spread over her immaculate pearl grey lapels. A hush hung over the school as we stared in horror at what he'd done. Even Donald was scared and ran home as fast as he could. Miss Leppard, all but burst into tears and she too ran home, but returned a little later without her precious gown, but much calmer. I can't remember what punishment followed this, but I am sure it warranted an entry in the Punishment Book.

When the audience had settled and it was time to begin, all the children, except the Queen and her entourage, lined up round the empty throne, tallest at the back, little ones at the front. The 'Royal Party' waited outside, then at a signal from Miss Leppard the children began to chant, in a whisper at first, but getting progressively louder until they were shouting; "We want a queen, we want a queen, WE WANT A QUEEN!"

Miss Leppard would then strike up with a pretty song called "May, oh lovely, smiling May." on the piano. This was the signal for the Queen and her attendants to enter. She would sit on her throne and the children would then sing the words to this song, which as far as I know was exclusive to Great Stukeley School.

May, o lovely, smiling May,
Come with beauty light and flowers,
With light and flowers.
We would welcome thee today.
So greet with joy, o greet with joy,
Thy fragrant hours.

When this song had been sung, a boy bearing a cushion on which the crown was set, stepped forward, bowed to the Queen and to the audience.

The Lady in Waiting (usually the Queens best friend) then stepped forward and taking the crown from the cushion, placed it on the Queen's head.

"I crown thee Queen of the May!" She declared loudly.

The biggest boy in the school, then stepped forward and demanded.

"Three cheers for the Queen of the May!"

Children and audience duly obliged.

Miss Leppard then played the tune again as the children paid homage to their Queen by filing past and bowing or curtsying. The boys, uncomfortable in their Sunday best and slicked back Brylcreemed hair, would take this opportunity to stick out their tongues at the Queen as they bowed. She would try desperately to look regal whilst trying to suppress her giggles.

This ritual over we went through our repertoire of May Day songs, which included "Hush there's the Rustling of Silken Dresses.", "The Floral Dance", "Jockey to the Fair." and "Come Lassies and Lads."

After this came the recitations, songs and instrumental solos or duets, which was followed by a performance by the Percussion Band. We had been rehearsing for weeks a selection of nursery rhymes and safety first songs. There were all kinds of instruments. The little children shook pieces of wood with a bell fastened to each end, older girls played the tambourine and cymbals, but only boys played the drums, of which there were several sizes. The most boring instrument was to my mind the triangle.

After the tea interval, during which we had to listen to the speeches, we had maypole dancing. Two of the heaviest boys had to stand at the base of this ancient fertility symbol, because it used to sway dangerously on the uneven wooden floor. Sometimes this was erected in the playground, if the weather was good enough.

We eight black-plimsoll girls (occasionally a boy as well) would skip round to the old familiar tunes (Floral Dance and Come Lassies and Lads) thumped out on the piano by Miss Leppard. Holding our blue and white ribbons aloft we would weave in and out creating intricate patterns down the shaft of the maypole. When our ribbons were all used up, we paused in order for the audience to admire our work, (but also to get our breath back) then off we would go again, unwinding our ribbons until we stood once more, red faced and breathless and ready to create another pattern to another tune.

The wonderful day came to an end when the local photographer, Mr. Ernest Whitney, took pictures of the May Queen and her attendants and the performers. Much to our delight, Mr. Whitney always called our teacher 'Miss Leopard'. When we pointed this out to her she was very cross and threatened to have us write out her name and the name of the animal a hundred times, so that we would see the difference. I rather think she would have liked to give Mr. Whitney a similar punishment!

The very last ritual of the day was the cutting of the special cake that was adorned with the May Queen's name. This was performed by the Queen with due ceremony and all the children had a slice. Any that was left over the Queen could take home. Then it was all over and there was nothing left for us but to wend our way home.

The next day we cleared up the drooping flowers and tidied up the schoolroom and the Queen was once more an ordinary schoolgirl.

However, the memories of those golden days have remained with me so strongly though the years that I only have to catch the scent of lilac to be transported back to that dusty little schoolroom and I experience again the sights, sounds and smells of those magical May days and I smile as I recall the time when I was queen for a day!

THE FETE

Village Fete
VJ Day 1945

Every year the village held a Garden Fete. Mostly this was held in and around the W.I.Hall. This stood on the edge of The Park, so the stalls were set up on the grass just beyond the fence that surround the Hall, but refreshments were served, as always, inside the building.

There were lots of stalls offering all kinds of entertainment and goodies. Hoop la! was popular, but I was never very good at hand/eye coordination, so I didn't waste my pennies on that. I always felt sure that the rings were far too small to encircle the prize anyway! I spent most of my money on the Roll A Penny stall, which was all luck and very little judgement! Other prizes could be won by throwing darts at playing cards fixed to a board.. The higher the card one pierced the better the prize. I loved the Bran Tub, where everyone won something as we dived our hands into the barrel of saw dust and felt around until we found something of interest. There was also the exciting Treasure Hunt. This was a piece of turf that was divided into many tiny squares. We then purchased a stick, wrote our name on it and stuck it in one of the squares hoping that it was the one designated as containing the 'treasure' a (ten shilling note). I never won this, although dreams of such riches made me want to invest in more than one square.

Then there was Bowling For The Pig. I'm not sure how this worked, but the prize was a little live piglet. I used to have a go, but what Mum would have thought had I won this prize I don't know! If I had won it, then there was no doubt that it would have ended up as a pet, because even though meat was rationed, all our chickens, ducks and rabbits died of old age after living on the fat of the land for all of their lives. No one in the family would have eaten an ex pet, even if one of my parents had managed to pluck up courage to kill one.

I loved poking about on the White Elephant stall and sometimes, much to Mum's dismay, purchased a cheap piece of rubbish that caught my eye. I am told that in a part of India white elephants are sacred and revered almost as gods, so that, while being given one as a gift was a great honour, it was also a burden, because it couldn't be made to work, but it still had to be fed and looked after. Hence the White Elephant stall sold things that were useless! Mum would have agreed with that!

More to Mum's taste was the Bring and Buy stall, whereby she could take along something we didn't particularly like or want, and buy something more to her taste. The Bottle Stall was the same and one could purchase a bottle of sauce, lemonade, beer or suchlike for a very small price, because all the goodies had been donated.

Naturally, Gill and I always saved a few coppers for the Refreshments, which was good value, especially if we helped out by collecting up the dirty cups and saucers, or tidying the tables. This could earn us an egg and cress sandwich, a slice of her Mum's sponge cake or a piece of my Mum's shortbread or a jam tart. We knew which home made cakes and tarts to avoid like the plague. It was easy to recognize Mrs. P-S's jam tarts, for they were grey, hard and had a mere smear of jam in them! Certainly not for us, although it was quite good fun floating them on saucers of tea ... they never sunk!

If you were to have asked Mum if she had any artistic talents she would have denied it emphatically, but she was wrong, for not only was she an expert at making wedding and birthday cakes and decorating them, she could also create a fancy dress costumes out of practically nothing and her designs invariably won a prize for my sisters. I wasn't ever keen on getting dressed up, so I didn't often enter for these events.

The most successful of these Fancy Dress competitions was the one held to celebrate VJ in 1945. The Fete that year was held in the grounds of Great Stukeley Hall and not the W.I. Hall as was usually the case. The entrants for the Fancy Dress Parade gathered on the Terrace. It was cold, wet and windy, but there was a good turn out. I have a picture of the occasion, supplied by my friend Gill Brown (nee Curtis) and looking at it now takes me right back to that day when we celebrated the Victory over our then enemy, Japan.

I was (for once) dressed in a colourful (and authentic) Hungarian Gypsy outfit lent to me by Mrs. Gilmour. My friends Iris and Gill were a Flower Girl and a Bride respectively; there was a sprinkling of Crinoline Ladies (Shirley Cannon and Anita Sly), Dutch Girl (Sheila Smith), Red Riding Hood (Sheila Marshall), a topical Britannia (Elizabeth Haynes), a delightful Miss Muffett , complete with large spider sewn onto her skirt, and carrying a stool (Marian Tasker), and little Margaret Cannon is memorable for shivering and with teeth chattering in her scanty Belly Dancers outfit!

Amongst the boys there were a couple of clowns (John Lovell and Brian Smith), A sailor and a Robin Hood (Laurence and Derek Burton) a Chinaman (Ivan Cannon), a pirate (Brian Clayton) and a cute, shy little Red Indian (Raymond Cade). However the winners were my sisters Marion and Irene, who were Sunshine and Showers. Marion wore a white dress with irregular grey patches to symbolize clouds and dabs from the blue bag to represent the sky. She wore a pointed hat from which streamed shredded cellophane, that cascaded over her shoulders to the hem of her skirt, this was the rain. Irene wore yellow with a gold sunray headdress, gold sequins were scattered over her dress. They held a cardboard rainbow supported by canes between them. It was an original and pretty design and deserved to win.

Another of Mum's original ideas for another occasion was making a three tiered wedding cake out of cardboard and white crepe paper, decorated with silver horseshoes and flowers. This was recycled for another fete and made into a birthday cake by removing a couple of layers and adding some pink decorations. The designs won both times.

I have memories of another Fete held in The Park just after the war. Betty Porter, who lived in College Farm after the Claytons left, brought along two fat little ponies and was letting children pay a copper or two for rides on these placid animals along a measured stretch of turf.

Gill and I had declared ourselves 'horse mad' and had even discussed whether it was worth asking our parents for a real live horse for Christmas. We had never been on horse (or pony) back before, but felt sure that we would be expert at this. So we paid Betty our coppers and she said she'd help us get on.

I was wearing a skirt (no jeans or trousers for girls in those days) and climbing aboard the wide back of the pony was not as easy as it looked, for as soon as I got in the saddle, I began to slip down the other side. Betty tried to stabilise me, but I found it almost impossible to do as she said and hold the reins and keep upright. Eventually, I managed to get astride the beast and sat straight. Betty said a quiet "Walk on!" to the pony and that is where my troubles really began! It had always looked so easy when I saw Betty and other experts riding, but it was just about the most uncomfortable thing I had ever done. I would rise in the stirrups only to find the pony had gone down, then I'd come down and meet the ponies wide back with a tooth-jarring thump. Then I began to slip off yet again. I did manage to get back to base without actually falling off, but it was touch and go. I decided there and then that horse riding was undignified, dangerous, painful and definitely not for me! I can't remember how Gill got on, she probably got on just fine, although I think we both stopped asking for things like horses for Christmas!

All the village turned out to support the Fete and as it usually ended with a dance in the W.I.Hall in the evening, everyone was catered for.

The proceeds went towards Children's Christmas Party or a summer trip to either Wicksteed Park or one of the East Coast seaside town, nearly always Hunstanton or Skegness.

I loved the Fete and in an era when entertainment wasn't readily available, it gave us something to look forward to.

That the Village Fete is still popular today proves that it has lasting appeal. I know we thought that Great Stukeley had the best … and looking back, I'm sure we did.

THE CONCERT

At regular intervals in the years immediately after the war, a concert would be staged in the W.I. Hall. I don't know who organised these affairs and rehearsed the cast, but the same people appeared in every one of them, and it was something to be looked forward to with excitement.

I am sure they were staged in the winter months, because I have vivid memories of leaving the hot and smoky hall and walking home in the cold frosty night air.

On the day of the concert, Miss Leppard finished school early. We older children had to carry the school chairs that were loaned for the performance, up to the hall, one or at the most, two at a time. This was hard work and very time consuming because it was quite a long walk, especially when encumbered with a chair, so several rests were needed along the way.

The W.I. Hall had been transformed by erecting a small stage at the 'ladies' end of the building so that the cramped little cloakroom could be used as a dressing room for the performers. A curtain was hung across the stage, and with a lot of imagination one could believe that we were in a real theatre.

The chairs we had hauled from the school were drawn up into rows, those from the Little Room at the front, so children could sit on them.

The excitement was intense as we assembled for our 'one night only' show. We filed into the hall, paying our shilling to the lady who sat at a green baize covered card table by the door, with a roll of tickets, which she dished out with aplomb.

I had to sit on the front seats as they were the ones allotted to children, but they were not very comfortable, especially if one was 'tall for one's age' (which I was!). However, it was worth it for the magical evening that lay ahead of us.

Everything about the concert filled me with anticipation and excitement, leaving home on a cold dark night, the fun of seeing familiar villagers dressed up and looking so different in stage make-up and clothes cavorting about on the stage. Then there were the tasty refreshments (Gill and I hoping for egg and cress sandwiches!), the raffle for simple prizes and finally singing all the familiar choruses along with the cast.

The format of these concerts was much the same for every

performance. It always began with the whole company on stage singing a selection of jolly songs, well known enough for everyone to join in. This got the audience warmed up and there followed a variety of 'turns' and sketches, some funny, some sad and some dramatic.

An elderly resident (I seem to think he may have lived for a while in Denmark House), Mr. Sutton, grey suited and grey haired, always recited a monologue, with The Green Eye Of The Little Yellow God and Gunga Din being amongst his favourites.

Mr. Waldock, stout, red faced and jolly, and Mr. Wilson, thin, pale faced and serious looking (their contrast in appearance couldn't have been more marked) always sang a comic duet. One that springs to mind is I'm A Little Prairie Flower, during which these two gentlemen, stalwarts of village society, pranced about on stage dressed as flowers, much to everyone's amusement.

One year the W.I. Drama group performed a sketch called 'Aunt Matilda's Collar'. Mrs. Wilson played the title role and Mrs. Waldock was her maid, accused of losing the lace collar in question, which she hotly and tearfully denied. When Aunt Matilda rose from her chair to admonish the maid, the audience could clearly see the collar attached to her skirt. Neither she, nor her maid could. I am sure there was a lot of 'Look behind you!' from the children, in time honoured fashion, before the problem was resolved. I can remember I thought it was hilarious.

Mrs. Gillett, the Baptist Lay Preacher's wife, her plump body encased in tight blue satin, would then sing The Holy City in her strong and piercing soprano voice. One year her pixie faced little son Raymond, joined in with her from the body of the hall, completely unrehearsed. He was familiar with the song from listening to his mother practice at home. This brought forth many ahhs and oohs from the adults in the audience.

Her stocky, curly haired husband would then join her on stage and they would sing a duet or two in the style of Anne Zeigler and Webster Booth, the well known duettists so popular on radio in those days. I recall a spirited rendering of 'The Keys Of Heaven' and 'Oh, No John, No John No!' He looking as romantic as he could and she, trying to look coy, which wasn't easy for a plump lady, with round owl-like glasses and Marcel waved hair, her face red from her exertions. Gill also recalls being fascinated because of the spittle that formed at the corners of her mouth.

When his wife left the stage, Mr. Gillett would sing his solos, a romantic number then something stirring and patriotic like Rose Of England. The Gilletts usually ended their set with another light hearted duet, probably a song from an Ivor Novello musical or a comic opera.

My friend Jean Cox's older sister, Barbara, dressed in smart topper and tails and looking very glamorous, along with Vivian Prior dressed as a bride, sang a jolly version of Me and My Gal.

During the interval the usual refreshments were served by the usual W.I. Ladies and a few modest prizes were raffled. People took this opportunity to stand outside and cool down, because by now the hall was hot, stuffy and full of cigarette smoke, for most men smoked and quite a lot of women did too.

The second half of the concert was much the same as the first, although one year a minor sensation was caused by a young woman from Huntingdon, not a regular performer, who must have been a friend of one of the cast. She was sitting at a table on stage, singing to a photograph of a serviceman in uniform with great feeling. The song 'I Never Said Thanks For That Lovely Week-end' was popular at the time and very poignant in the aftermath of a war. During her rendition her fashionably short skirt rode up and the audience was presented with a fine view of her pretty crepe de chine French knickers! Much laughter and ribald comments were heard at the end of the show. Although I didn't understand much of what was said, I did find the image of this lady showing off her knickers very funny.

Jean Cox, Iris Turton and I longed to perform in the concert, so Jean asked Barbara if we could. She told us to choose suitable songs and practice and apply when they were next going to rehearse. We took this advice very seriously and decided for some reason to sing 'Carolina In The Morning' and 'California Here I Come'. Iris also practiced many show tunes on her accordion, alas to no avail. We were never asked to perform, so who knows what loss to show business this might have been!

One year a concert party from a neighbouring village (Brampton, I think) who called themselves The Rainbows put on a show for us. They were better rehearsed, more professional and had a bigger cast than our village effort, but it wasn't the same without the familiar village people and their routines. I don't think the village ever put on another show, which was shame, because whether the adults in the audience enjoyed it or not, to the children it was a wonderful occasion and an exciting break from routine in those bleak, colourless days just after the war.

WHIST DRIVES

Whist Drives were very popular in Great Stukeley during the 1940s and early 50s and were well attended. They were held in the W.I. Hall on alternate Friday evenings throughout the winter months.

Before I was allowed to accompany Mum on to these events, she would go on her own, whilst Dad looked after me and the twins and vice versa.

I would hear them talking at Saturday morning breakfast and was mystified by the tales of …'she was leading trumps ..' or ' … can you believe it, she actually trumped her partners ace!' and other unforgivable sins committed at the card table the night before. I had no idea what it was all about, but it sounded interesting.

I was about ten when I was allowed to go along with Mum and I expect she enjoyed my company on the long walk down the lane to our house on those dark winter evenings. I didn't have to go to school the next day, so going to bed late was not a problem.

My very good friend Gill Curtis used to come along with her mother, who was caretaker of the W.I. Hall and a leading light in the Women's Institute, for it was they that organised the Whist Drives, I think, and the profits made went towards a Christmas party and outings to Wicksteed Park in the summer.

Gill and I weren't expert enough to join in with the serious card players, but we really enjoyed these evenings together and would erect a card table in the corner by the ladies cloakroom and play our own card games, a favourite being a simple version of the main game called Knock-Out Whist and we would try and keep our inevitable giggling down so as not to distract the card players who were intent on winning one of the very modest prizes on offer.

Sometimes we would get tired of playing cards and we would just talk, mostly about the latest books we were reading, for both Gill and I were avid readers and swapped and shared any books we had for birthdays or Christmas, for we both enjoyed adventure stories.

One night , Gill and I got ourselves into deep trouble. One of the regular card players brought along her young daughter

Sheila, who was a couple of years younger than Gill. We were asked if this child could join us in our games. This didn't actually thrill us, because Sheila was a whining and miserable child and given to bursting into tears at the slightest provocation. However, we said she could sit with us throughout the evening, not that we had much choice in the matter.

Sheila didn't know how to play cards and didn't want to watch us play, so we decided to embark on another of our favourite pastimes, making up our own stories. We decided that we were going to tell a ghost story. I can't remember the details of this un-doubtedly gory tale, but during the telling of it we told Sheila that the Ladies Cloakroom just behind us, was haunted. We went on to relate a long and involved tale of an unfortunate lost soul con-demned to spend eternity closeted (if you'll excuse the pun!) in the tiny W.I. Ladies loo!

To our surprise and delight, Sheila believed us and was terri-fied! We were amazed that anyone could take such nonsense seriously, but she did and went crying to her mother, complaining that Gill and I had scared her.

Her mother, furious at having her card game interrupted and having her little girl upset, came storming over to us and gave us a good telling off for scaring her child. Our own mothers came over and demanded to know if we had tried to frighten her. We admitted it and had to apologise to both Sheila and her mother. This didn't help to make us warm to the child, who spent the rest of the evening glued to her mother's side. I doubt whether her whining and grizzling made her popular with the other card play-ers, but at least we were free of her. The good thing to come out of this affair was that Sheila never came to another Whist Drive, for which Gill and I were extremely grateful!

Naturally, the best part of the evening for Gill and me was re-freshment time, when sandwiches and home made cakes were served along with tea poured from the big brown enamel teapots. As usual, our mothers were responsible for this and we knew which sponge cakes and jam tarts were made by Mum and Mrs. Curtis and our other friend's mothers and we knew equally well which ones to avoid, because not all W.I. Members were good cooks! We adored the egg and cress sandwiches and since most villagers kept a few hens, eggs were plentiful and cheap and bread wasn't then rationed, so we could usually rely on a good supply of egg sandwiches (with or without cress) and we often had the pleasure of 'clearing up' any that were left over. Gill and I were scrupulously fair about the division of spoils, even cutting a sandwich or jam tart in half if necessary.

To look at Gill one wouldn't think that she enjoyed such an 'healthy appetite', for she was about eighteen months younger than me and a few inches shorter and very slim and her appearance was completely at odds with her capacity for food. She was an attractive child, with straight dark, shiny hair and wide dark blue eyes. She had a ready smile and a sunny nature and although an only child, she was generous and wasn't in the least spoiled. We got along extremely well together and in all the years we were friends, I don't think we ever had a cross word or 'fell out' as most children do. We shared a silly sense of humour, were the greatest gigglers in the school and our love of reading and books sealed our friendship.

The second half of the Whist Drive ended with the presentation of the prizes by the person in charge, called the M.C., for he was the one who told the players where to move to after each hand. There was a rule that losing ladies stayed put, but winning gentlemen moved round to the right. This may not have been the way it was, but it was something like that, but I never really got the hang of this strange ritual, but most players seemed to circumnavigate the hall during the evening. Neither could I understand why sometimes Mum won a 'gents' prize. It was all to do with there being more ladies than men players, so some ladies had to play as men. The only drawback to this was that Mum might win a prize meant for a man. Shaving soap or pipe tobacco!

All the prizes were very modest , maybe talc for a woman or a small household item. There was always a Booby Prize for the player with the worst hand of all. This could be a box of matches or a packet of razor blades.

Any whole cakes that weren't eaten were auctioned off at the end of proceedings and there was always a raffle, with again a modest prize for the holder of the winning ticket.

Whist Drives were very well attended and their popularity certainly wasn't because of the players hope of winning one of the modest prizes, for no one would have left the warmth of their hearth and home on a cold winter night in order to win a tablet of soap. No, it must simply have been the pleasure of a hand or two of cards in the company of friends and neighbours that drew them there … Gill and I liked the egg sandwiches too!

THE
AMERICANS

It was with great excitement that we heard about the 'American Invasion' of our little village during the early 1940s and it was soon to make a huge difference to our lives in Owls End, for the usually quiet lane became busy with the constant toing and froing of what we called 'Yankie' lorries, jeeps and cars.

Great Stukeley Hall, the big house at the centre of the Estate, was requisitioned and turned into an American Officer's Billet, whose elite residents were looked after by an army of cooks, waiters, valets and other men who were there to do the menial tasks for their superiors, so it wasn't surprising that the place hummed with activity.

As well as this, right at the end of the lane, behind my friend Jean's thatched cottage, was a small contingent of G.I.s, who lived in a couple of Nissen huts and whose purpose was to man an anti-aircraft gun, that sat menacingly in a large hole in the middle of the field that surrounded the cottage. One of the Nissen huts was a cook-house and mess hall, the other was a dormitory, where the men slept.

The purpose of the gun was to protect the Alconbury Base, which was not far away as the crow flies, but I don't think it was ever fired in anger. There is no doubt that we would have heard it if it had, for it was large and impressive looking weapon. The hole in which it was housed was called The Gun Site by both the men who looked after it and the villagers.

The men who guarded this gun were obviously very bored, for there was little to do, so they seemed to welcome chatting to Jean and me when we visited them in their hole in the ground. I suppose that even our childish chatter was a break from the monotony and idleness of sitting beside the gun as it crouched there covered with camouflage netting.

They were a very nice bunch of young men, but there was one in particular who was our favourite. Hilly was a tall, gangly lad, with a strange (at least to our ears) accent. He didn't sound like the film stars we had seen on our rare visits to the cinema, but had a slow, country drawl that probably originated from one of the Southern States. He always had his guitar with him and needed very little encouragement to strum it and sing a selection of 'cowboy' songs to us. I have no idea if he was any good, but to Jean and me he sounded wonderful. He would teach us the words to some of the songs and we would join in the choruses. He told us that he had written some of the songs himself and I have no reason to disbelieve him, because I have never heard them before or since. I still remember the words and the very simple tune to one of them.

Live and let live,
Don't break my heart,
Don't leave me here to die.
I never could live if we should part,
To part would mean goodbye.

Not very original words, but we loved to sing along with Hilly and his guitar.

One day after he had finished his shift at the Gun Site, Hilly asked us if we would like some chewing gum and candy. Naturally, we said yes please, for we loved American candy, deprived as we were of sweets, since they were on ration, so the chance of some extra candy was very exciting.

Hilly explained that he would have to go to his billet in the Nissen Hut to get the goodies and asked us to walk over there with him. This wasn't something that we had done before and we felt very grown up when we were allowed to go into the cookhouse/mess hall to wait for him, while he went to his room to get the candy.

Where we sat at one of the tables, we could see into the kitchen area, and I was horrified to see a cook, in gleaming white uniform, wielding a huge knife as he sliced up great quantities of bloody meat on a wooden block. The thing that was most scary to me was that the cook was an inscrutable looking Oriental gentleman and I (brought up on wartime propaganda) was convinced that this man must be a JAP! How was it possible that these Americans hadn't noticed that he had infiltrated their ranks (for he was obviously a spy) and was surely up to no good at all! I was convinced that any moment, Jean and I would be chopped up with the piles of meat he was slicing.

It was with great relief that I saw Hilly come back into the room carrying the promised gum and candy. We thanked him and I couldn't wait to get outside and away from that sinister looking man. I can't remember if I voiced my fears to Jean, but I know it worried me for a long time afterwards. Poor man! He was probably Chinese or Filipino, but to me, who had never seen an Oriental person in the flesh before, he had to be Japanese and therefore The Enemy. I never saw him again, so convinced myself that they had discovered what he was up to and he had been imprisoned ... or worse!

Americans have the reputation for being friendly and this was certainly true of the lads that worked at The Hall and on the Gun Site. We didn't get to meet many of the officers who lived in the former, but many of the staff that looked after them became firm friends with my family and other people in the village.

Village women used to do the laundry for the G.I.s. I don't know how much they paid for this service, but it wasn't exactly easy money in the days before washing machines and electric irons, but whatever they were paid, it was a welcome supplement to our meagre income. My mother did washing for one or two of these Americans and that was how we got to know them.

My parents were always hospitable and the G.I.s (many of whom were away from home for the first time) seemed to appreciate being accepted into our family, for it must have eased their homesickness a little.

The first Yank (as we always affectionately called them) we got to know was a tall, dark young man called Eddie Deal. He was extremely handsome and his film star good looks made him very popular with the local girls. Unfortunately, he was arrogant and vain as well and although besotted with Betty, our friend from Lawn Cottages next door to us, she wasn't in the least interested in him, which he couldn't understand at all and it only served to make him more persistent.

I wasn't all that keen on Eddie, but then he hardly ever spoke to me and was far too interested in himself and his looks to bother with being chatty or amusing to a child. He didn't endear himself to Mum either, for when he came to collect his laundry one day he asked if he could change into a clean shirt at our house, because he was off out on a date. She said he could, then was dismayed to see him polishing up his shoes on one of our clean towels! This did not go down well and he couldn't understand why she was so cross with him.

My favourite Yank was a slightly older man who we knew only as Seniors. I am not sure if that is how he spelt his name, but that was the way we pronounced it. It was his surname and I don't think we ever knew his first name.

Seniors was probably in his late twenties or early thirties and was of medium height, stocky and with a beat-up, but kindly sort of face. He was also very funny. He liked nothing better than to spend any off duty evenings he had with us, playing cards or darts with Dad, or just sitting around chatting.

For some reason he always called me Janet. I think it was because he knew someone at home who looked like me with that name, but whatever the reason, he never called me anything else.

Seniors had the ability to make me laugh until I cried, which to be honest wasn't hard to do, but he had a way of saying things in exactly the way that set me off giggling. I adored him, for he was like a kind hearted and amusing uncle.

I am not sure what Seniors's duties were at the Hall, but I think he must have been a steward or cook. Whatever his job was, it entailed looking after the Officers and their food, which was very fortunate for us!

One warm summers evening my family and I were sitting around listening to the radio and reading and doing all the sort of things we used to do to amuse ourselves, when there was a knock at the back door.

On opening it, Mum was delighted to find Seniors and a colleague standing there with several plates in their arms. They swept into our kitchen and with a flourish removed the napkins to reveal plates piled high with cold chicken salad, potato salad and even bread rolls and butter. There was one for each of us. It appeared that during a dinner party for the Officers, an opportunity had arisen for Seniors to 'liberate' some spare meals for his English friends. It was such a treat for us, all the more for being unexpected. The chicken was tender and succulent, the salad was crisp and the potato salad was delicious. There were even little pots of mayonnaise on the side. We only had chicken on high days and holidays, so it was even more of a treat than it would be today.

Seniors and his friend couldn't stay, for they had to get back to work, so they each made a deep bow and made to go.

"Just a minute." Dad said. "You forgot something. Where's the salt and pepper!"

Most people in the village kept a few hens or ducks, which were a valuable source of eggs and meat. The ration of one egg per person per week was hardly adequate, so to have one's own supply was desirable, if not essential. When the hens were laying well, Mum would preserve any surplus eggs in a large container filled with a liquid she called 'water glass', which kept them in reasonably good condition for some time. Our chickens were never killed, because my parents were too soft hearted, so our hens lived to a ripe old age, whether they were laying or not! Chickens for Christmas dinner were bought from less squeamish neighbours, although Mum didn't mind plucking and drawing them.

Although food was strictly rationed for us, the Yanks had more than they could eat and the wastage at the Hall was phenomenal. Our friends in the kitchen there would save all the scraps in a large wooden chest and bring it over to our house so that we could feed it to our chickens. The chest had a lid and occasionally, the men would say, with a knowing wink, "Don't be too long opening the chest, otherwise the stuff inside might go off."

As soon as they'd gone Mum would look in the chest and find something interesting buried beneath the food scraps. It might be a large can of lean and delicious corned beef (quite different from the corned beef we were used to), a tin of fruit salad, or maybe a sealed container with a wonderful lemon meringue pie inside it, but best of all was when we found a sealed metal container that held a most delicious concoction of ice cream with chunks of pineapple embedded in it. Absolutely wonderful!

These little treats were almost certainly illegal, but they, without doubt helped to cement Anglo-American relations in our household, for in return we could offer them a little bit of family life, which was a relief from the austere barrack room existence they endured most of the time.

All American servicemen, whether we knew them or not, were exceedingly generous to English children during those wartime days and it was not unknown for men being transported in the back of Yankie lorries to throw out handfuls of candy and chewing gum to any children they saw.

Some kids would shout out, "Got any gum, chum?" to any Yank that they saw, but we would not have dared to do so, for we were told it was rude and greedy to do that.

In these cautious times there is often a dark side to children being offered sweets by strangers and mothers would blanche at the thought of it now, but back then it was never regarded as anything sinister, the American servicemen offered and we accepted gratefully.

However, I did give my poor mother a scare one day.

One fine summer's day when my sisters were about four and I was eight, we were dawdling home from school along Owls End, having been seen across the road by Mrs. Waldock as usual. We had walked a little way up the lane, when a jeep stopped beside us. It contained a round little officer and his driver. The officer got out and started chatting to us. He asked our names and where we lived. He crouched down and chatted to the twins, obviously entranced by their blonde cuteness.

He then asked me if it would be all right if he took them up to the Hall to his quarters, because he would like to give them some candy. I said it would be OK and he lifted them into his jeep and away they went.

I was happy to wend my way home on my own, for it meant I could look for birds nests here, pick a few flowers there, stop and look at the calves at the farm and generally please myself.

I eventually arrived home, wandered in and was met by my worried mother. The following conversation ensued.

Mum: You're late. Where are the twins?

Me: They went off in a jeep.

Mum: (looking worried) When?

Me: A little while ago.

Mum: Who was in the jeep?

Me: A Yank.

Mum: Which one?

Me: Don't know.

Mum: Wasn't he one of those we know?

Me: No, I've never seen him before.

Mum: (very worried by now) What did he say?

Me: He wanted to give them some sweets. What's for tea?

Mum: (getting cross as well as worried now) Never mind tea. Just tell me what he looked like.

Me: Don't know. I've forgotten.

Mum: Why on earth did you let them go with him?

Me: Because he wanted to give them some sweets.

Mum: (grasping me by the shoulders) Which way did they go?

Me: To the Hall, I think.

I could see that Mum was getting really cross with me by now, although I really couldn't see why or what I had done that was so wrong. It seemed like a lot of fuss over nothing.

"Come on," she said. "We'll have to go and look for them."

She grabbed my hand and dragged me out into the lane and along the drive that led to the Hall.

Suddenly, she breathed a sigh of relief, for coming into view was the tubby little officer (beaming from ear to ear) with a delighted twin on each hand, both of them laden with a bag of candy bars.

He smiled at my mother a little sheepishly.

"I guess I should apologise, Ma'm. " He said. "But I couldn't resist them, they looked so cute and reminded me of my kids at home. I just had to stop and get them a mite of candy, I didn't stop to think that you might be concerned, but then I expect your daughter explained, didn't she?"

"Of course," Mum said, giving my hand a squeeze.

He told the twins to be sure and share their candy with their big sister, then stopping only to ruffle their hair, he left and returned to the Hall. We never saw him again.

Luckily, no harm was done, but I got strict instructions that I was never to let them go off with strangers again. I thought it was all a big fuss over nothing and couldn't understand why Mum had been so worried, after all, hadn't I told her that the officer had only wanted to give them candy. He was a very kind man, that's all. Now, of course, I can see only too well what thoughts were running through my mother's mind!

The Americans were always good to English children, but at Christmas they excelled themselves, for they put on a wonderful party at the Alconbury Base, to which all the village children were invited.

The khaki-coloured lorries with the familiar white star emblazoned on their side would go around the village picking up children and taking them, to what seemed to us, wonderland.

On arrival at the base, the lorries would be met by a line of G.I.s and as we children alighted, we would be greeted by one of the men and they would be our 'uncle' for the duration of the party. It was his job to make sure that the child in his care had the time of their life.

My friend Jean and I went to one of these parties, although I can't be sure which year it was, although I believe it to be 1942 or 1943. When we got off the lorry we were befriended by two buddies (as they called themselves), who introduced themselves to us as Walter and Bill. They were both good-looking, in the style of Clark Gable, with neatly clipped moustaches. They were so charming, warm and friendly that we were both equally smitten!

They told us that they were gunners who flew in the planes that went on missions to bomb Germany and the first thing they did was to show us round the plane. Walter (my 'uncle') showed me the 'bubble' at the rear that was his position and as young as I was at the time, I can still remember how horrified I felt on realising how vulnerable and claustrophobic it must have been during flights over enemy territory.

The two men showed us round all kinds of interesting places on the base, which was like a foreign land to us. Then they took us into the large Nissen Hut where the party was held. Here we saw rows of trestle tables drawn up and covered with white cloths and set with plates, cups and cutlery. This was the canteen and we were taken up to the counter where rows of cooks in sparkling white uniforms helped to serve us with a variety of food we hadn't seen for ages. There were slices of cold roast chicken, ham, corned beef (lean and delicious and not at all like we were used to). There were chips, hot potatoes, potato salad, hot vegetables, cold salad, cheeses, hot dogs, and piles of delicious bread, spread thickly with real butter (a whole weeks ration on one slice!). Then there were the cakes, lemon meringue pie, fruit salads with tiny little marshmallows in it, doughnuts, creamy ice cream and frosted Christmas cakes made of a light and fluffy sponge, not like the heavy fruit cakes our mothers had been saving their dried fruit for months to make. To wash it down we had the choice of lemonade, orange juice, milk or a curious fizzy brown drink in an odd shaped bottle that they called 'coke', which was something completely new to us.

This feast left us wide-eyed with wonder, for we were allowed to eat as much as we liked and many went back for seconds and even thirds!

After we had eaten our fill, Santa came into the room laden with a bulging sack. He handed out gifts to every child in the room. Most were toys made by the G.I.s in their spare time. Each child received a wooden replica of the ubiquitous 'Yankie lorry', painted khaki with the familiar white star on the side. They were beautifully made and quite big and sturdily constructed. We loved them and my sisters and I each had one and played with it for many years. They were a marvellous souvenir of a momentous occasion.

The party ended with music and singing of carols, until it was time for our 'uncles' to take us back to the lorries that were taking us home.

I think we must have been given the address of our 'uncles', because I know both Jean and I wrote to Walter and Bill to thank them for a wonderful afternoon and we were thrilled when they took the trouble to write back. Walter's note was brief, telling me something about his life on base. We exchanged a few letters with them over the next few weeks, then one day I got one of my letters returned. Bill wrote to Jean and told her that Walter had been killed in action. I was very upset and thought then, as I do now, that to die in that little Perspex bubble at the rear of the plane, must have been sheer hell. I was very upset.

Remembering those two young men today, I think they must have been extremely nice lads, for they took the time to write notes to two little girls, whose letters in return must have been rather boring for them when they had far better things to do with their time.

One of the best Christmases I can remember as a child was the year we celebrated the Festive Season with a houseful of people. Usually, it was just Mum, Dad, the twins and me, but Christmas 1944 was different.

We had a couple of lodgers at the time. They were Mr. Martindale, a round, jolly little man with a bald head and infectious giggle and Ken Harrison, a good-looking young man with dark wavy hair and a charming manner. Mr. Martindale was the manager of a group of English civilian engineers employed by the USAAF and who worked on the Alconbury Base. Ken Harrison was one of his assistants. Both were from Preston in Lancashire and spoke with broad accents, quite unlike anything we had heard before.

Mr. Martindale was going home that Christmas, but Ken was on stand-by duty and had to stay in Great Stukeley, so he asked Mum if he could have his wife, Alwyn, come down to stay with us over the Christmas holidays. Ken's friend, Cliff, also an engineer from Preston, lodged with Mr. & Mrs. Hutson in the house next door and he had arranged for his wife to stay with him there, so the two women travelled down from Preston together, arriving on Christmas Eve.

One of our American friends from The Hall, Eddie du Becky, had recently broken off his engagement to an English girl and was at a loose end, so he too asked if he could spend Christmas Day with us. Mum always said that our house had elastic walls, so she agreed!

Alwyn stayed with Ken in the room that he usually shared with Mr. Martindale, Cliff and his wife Evelyn, slept at the Hutson's house, but spent the rest of the time with us.

Alwyn was a petite and pretty lady, who dressed very elegantly, with high heeled shoes and immaculate make-up, her dark curly hair always looked nice and she had a sweet and happy disposition. We liked her at once and she fitted in with us as if she had known us all her life.

Evelyn, was a fiery red-head, who never seemed to be content with her lot. She was moody and complained all the time about everything, she also hen pecked and nagged the quiet and unassuming Cliff unmercifully. She was not a happy girl. She couldn't have been more different from the sunny natured Alwyn.

Alwyn had long red nails and wore a heavy silver charm bracelet that jangled on her slender wrist. This item of jewellery fascinated me, for it had dozens of tiny charms on it. She would sometimes take it off so that I could look at it closely and she would tell me what each charm was and who had given it to her. There was a miniature Arabian slipper with upturned toe, a filigree jug, cats, dogs, teddy bears, bunnies, an oriental lamp and a little 'spinner' that had some odd symbols engraved on it, that spelt out the words 'I Love You' when spun. Another had the word MIZPAH engraved on it. Alwyn told me that this was an Arabic (I think) word that meant 'The Lord Be between Us When We Are Apart', which seemed an awfully long translation of one word to me! My favourite was a very pretty and ornate silver tassel. I loved that bracelet and longed to own one and promised myself that when I grew up I would buy one. Sadly, by the time I was able to afford to buy jewellery, my tastes had changed!

Mum was in her glory making all the arrangements for this party. She had been gathering together and saving various items that were rationed and organised a couple of cockerels from a neighbour. I remember that when the twins had an orange (on green ration books only, which were issued to young children) Mum saved the rind and 'candied' it (I have no idea how this was done) and it was then chopped and incorporated in both the pudding and a cake. I think I am right in saying that we were allowed slightly increased rations of some items for Christmas, although it was still very frugal.

I am sure that Ken and Alwyn brought stuff for the feast and of course, Eddie du Becky certainly did. Mum was very good at bartering for things she needed; a bag of potatoes for a chicken, a pound of sausages from someone who had had a pig killed, for a jar of bottled fruit and so forth. We had plenty of good fresh vegetables from the garden and lots of eggs from the chickens,

165

who thrived on their rich rations from the scraps left by the Officers at the Hall. All in all, we did very well and at Christmas Mum simply surpassed herself and we enjoyed wonderful food, which was such a treat, because these luxuries weren't available all year round like they are today.

Our chicken was a 'capon', which I think I am right in saying was a cockerel that had been castrated (chemically, I believe), which meant they grew large, meaty and very tasty and were delicious served with crispy golden roast potatoes, parsnips, Brussels Sprouts, carrots and the like, all grown from our own garden. I loved the bread sauce, that was creamy, spicy and utterly delicious, a perfect accompaniment to the succulent flesh of the bird. This was always followed by the dark, rich pudding that had been steaming for hours. Now we have exotic things like cream, brandy sauce, brandy butter and so forth, but then we were content with custard. The meal was never over for Dad, until he had a couple of mince pies, which had melt in the mouth pastry and Mum's homemade spicy mincemeat.

Eddie had supplied the more exotic goodies, like chocolates, delicious American cookies, nuts, Coca-Cola, a lemonade he called Seven Up, beer and a bottle of dark spirit that he called whisky, though it wasn't Scotch, but Bourbon. The alcohol was strictly for the adults, of course, but we kids loved the fizzy drinks and candy.

There were eight of us sitting round the big kitchen table for lunch that day, the five of us, plus Ken, Alwyn and Eddie. It was a jovial meal, with crackers, albeit flimsy wartime economy ones, that had all the usual paper hats, mottoes and corny jokes.

Around three o clock we were joined by Cliff and Evelyn, along with Cliff's landlady and her husband, who were our neighbours Mr. & Mrs. Hutson. They were a childless couple and Mum didn't like to think of them being on their own once Cliff and Evelyn joined us, so they had been invited too.

Once everyone had arrived and settled down, the real fun began.

Eddie had fixed a microphone in the kitchen and attached it to the radio in the front room, where everyone was sitting around chatting as we children played with our toys or read our books.

Suddenly, the radio crackled into life and out of it came a voice, loud and clear, announcing that Santa Claus was in the vicinity and would be calling upon the Wendholt Twins, Marion & Irene in the next few minutes. My little sister's eyes grew wide with amazement and excitement at hearing their names on the radio. They hadn't recognised the voice of Eddie as I had, but then I was old enough at nearly nine, to be let in on the secret.

Then we heard the jingling of 'sleigh bells' and a deep voice booming,

"Whoa! Steady you reindeer, we're here!"

The door opened and in walked Santa, complete with red coat and white whiskers. It was, Dad, of course, resplendent in an old red dressing gown and white cotton wool beard, but the twins truly thought it was the great man himself. Dad did a few unconvincing 'ho, ho, ho's' then greeted everyone in the room with a loud, "Merry Christmas, everyone!"

The sack he carried on his back was filled with all kinds of little parcels, which he promised to dish out if my sisters gave him a kiss. Marion dashed forward boldly, put her arms round his neck and kissed him warmly, but Irene was shy and had to be coaxed, but her big, baby-blue eyes opened even wider when he began to hand out the parcels.

The twins and I got our presents first, then there was one for everyone in the room and as he handed them out, he made appropriate remarks. For instance, to Mrs. Hutson, whose parcel contained a tablet of soap, he said. "May you hereafter lead a clean life." (as a devout Christian and regular churchgoer, this was thought to be doubly appropriate!). Cliff, whose gift was a pack of cigarettes, the wish was that all his troubles would go up in smoke. There was a joke for everyone, simple, but I suppose, in that rarefied atmosphere it seemed the height of wittiness!

After all the gifts had been allotted, Santa made his exit, with a fond farewell and much jingling of 'sleigh bells' (a length of chain in his pocket) and urging of the reindeer to "Giddy up!" he was gone.

After a while my father returned to the room as if nothing untoward had happened. My sisters hadn't even noticed that he was missing when Santa called.

The grown ups then chatted and laughed and the twins and I played with our toys until it was time for tea.

Mum served a selection of sandwiches, followed by more mince pies and a slice of the rich fruit cake that she had saved up the rations to make. It was all the more delicious because of the rarity of such luxury.

After tea, the women washed up and the scene was set for something I heard people in the house rehearsing, with much giggling, although I hadn't been allowed to see it.

This was the Shadow Play, which was performed by Dad, Ken, Cliff and Eddie. A white sheet was stretched across one half of the room and a bright light shone onto it from behind the performers, who were behind the sheet so that their shadows were thrown onto it.

The theme of the play was an operation.

Ken, the patient, lay on a table, where an anaesthetic was administered by way of a large mallet blow to the head. A huge saw was taken up and an incision made into the patient's abdomen, after which yards and yards of 'intestines' were pulled out (in reality a large roll of tape!) and eventually cut off with a huge set of garden shears. From time to time the patient would wake up, only to have another dose of the mallet administered. This went on for sometime and I considered it to be the funniest thing I had ever seen. Everyone was rolling about , but I was giggling so much it hurt!

All too soon the play was over and the props cleared away. We then sat round the fire, with the main lights turned out, so that the room was lit only by the flickering flames and we sang carols and the old familiar songs of Christmas that brought tears to the eyes of the grown ups as they remembered their own special Christmases in less troubled times.

Dad filled everyone's glass from his special bottle of Rich Red Ruby Port (or whatever an individual wanted) and proposed a toast to 'Absent Friends' and wished for a happier future with peace in the world.

Then it was over and reluctant to break the spell after such a perfect day, we climbed the stairs and scrambled into our beds, clutching hot water bottles, to take the chill off the sheets in our cold, unheated bedrooms.

It had been a wonderful Christmas and everyone who shared it with us said it was the best that they could remember. Even Eddie, who must have been homesick for his home and family in America, said it had been fun and one he would always remember. I wonder if he still recalls the English family in the small country village, the meal he shared with us and the laughter that was enjoyed by everyone all those years ago in wartime England.

We may not have had a lot of material goods in those days, but the warmth of the welcome extended to anyone who had nowhere to go was unrivalled, for no matter how many people we had in the house, there was always room 'for one more'!

The Yanks changed the life of the village a great deal. A lot of girls ended up as 'G.I. Brides, marrying their American boyfriends and going off to start a new life in a foreign land. Many thought it would be like it was in the movies and these were the ones that would return home disillusioned by it all. Thankfully, many were happy and enjoyed their life in the various States that they moved to.

We all thought Betty Allen would marry a Yank, for she was engaged to at least two, but she eventually married tall, dark, good-looking John Price, who lived in Little Stukeley, had a daughter, Kay and after a while moved to farm in (I think) Suffolk.

There were always jokes about the hopeful girls, who went steady with a G.I., applied to marry them and then spent months 'waiting for the papers to arrive', after their 'fiancé' had returned to America. In some cases, they are still waiting!

The Americans were kind and generous to children, so we loved them and were sorry to see them leave after the war. However, they weren't gone for long, because during the 1950s they were back at Alconbury and although there are only a handful left at the time of writing, they have been here ever since.

This 'occupation' has affected my family directly, for my sister Marion married her Californian, Rob Corley, in 1967 and thanks to her good taste in choosing someone from the San Francisco Bay Area, I have enjoyed a dozen perfect holidays with them during the past twenty years or so.

169

I miss my sister and her family very much, but it is a joy to be able to visit them, for I love them all dearly and California is beautiful!

The Americans influenced life in this country a great deal. Young women loved their exotic accents, their generosity, their charm and their fatter pay cheques and young men hated them for all the same things! However, I think on the whole they were a 'good thing'!

I never actually went out with a G.I. when I was a teenager, but several girls from my school did, married them and have settled happily in the U.S.A.. Their lives were certainly changed by the 'American Invasion' of the 1940s and onwards.

DAY TRIPS

Outing to Hunstanton on a rainy day. Circa 1949

Left to right:
Irene, Mum, Aunt Con, Marion and Old Mrs Sly

In background:
Mr & Mrs Owen

Holidays were very rare for us in the 1940s and 50s. We had to make do with day trips, rather than go off for a week long break.

I have many photographs of my family, taken with our little Box Brownie camera and by the ubiquitous beach and street photographers in the various East Coast resorts we visited, as records of these outings. My poor mother looks unhappy and anxious in every one of them. She admitted in later life she really hated these outings. My sister Irene, who suffered with travel sickness, was always ill on the coach, both going and coming home; one of us always fell over, or hurt ourselves in some way. Buckles would come off sandals, a dress would get torn and sand would get into the sandwiches she spent hours packing up for us. If the weather was hot she worried about us getting sunburned and if it rained she worried about what we would do all day. Money was short, so she had to keep a tight rein on what we could spend on ice creams and the fun fare. We were not allowed to visit the latter until late in the day, when we would be given our half a crown to spend. Rides were usually sixpence (two and a half pence in today's money), so the half a crown (twelve and a half pence) didn't go very far. I usually had one or two goes on the Galloping Horses and spent the rest on the penny slot machines, where one could win back a few pence, so that I could have more goes. The money always went, no matter how much I 'won'.

Sometimes it was possible to win a prize, always cheap rubbish, but one felt a sense of achievement to have a plastic comb, a cheap metal ring with a glass stone or a toffee as a trophy.

Many fathers worked on farms, so summertime, being their busiest time when they worked most daylight hours, was out of the question for outings. A lot of men folk were still in the forces, of course.

I quite liked the seaside trips, but they never turned out to be as good as I thought they would be. I expect Mum's anxiety and her fear that something awful would happen to one of us, probably transferred itself to me and took the edge off the excitement.

Something awful did happen to me once and I will never forget it.

We had gone to Lowestoft for our day trip, quite a change from the usual Hunstanton, Great Yarmouth or Skegness and somewhere we had never been before. The organisers of the event thought everyone would appreciate something different.

I was about fourteen years old and my sisters almost eleven. Although I can remember very little of the day, there was one episode that haunted me for years afterwards.

For once it had been a hot day and we had been on the beach for some time. My sisters had been in the sea, but I, not possessing a bathing suit was content to sunbathe on the beach in a deck chair next to Mum. I wore a cotton skirt and a rather fetching halter-necked top I had received courtesy of June Fenwick, the fashionable teenaged daughter of the Fenwick family who lived in Great Stukeley Hall. She often gave me her cast off clothing which I loved as it was always such good quality.

My sisters, not as self conscious as me, had each been splashing about in a pair of spare knickers taken along for that purpose.

As the twins dried off and put on their dry clothes, I mentioned to Mum that I would like to have a paddle before we went home. Mum suggested I put on a pair of Marion's knickers, which she had rinsed out before packing them into her bag, and have a quick dip before we departed for home. It was still very hot and the sea did look inviting, so I agreed. Under cover of a towel, I wriggled into the wet knickers with some difficulty; my desire to wade in the sea, overcoming my embarrassment at having to wear such an unflattering garment. I ran down to the water's edge as soon as I could and not wanting to show off my sister's underwear, I waded quite deep into the water, keen to hide them from view.

The tide was coming in, a brisk breeze had blown up, and the water became rather choppy. I waded out farther than I should have done. I felt the sand move beneath my feet and I began to feel unstable. Luckily, I was close to a break water, so I managed to grab onto it with one hand to steady myself. The water was really rough now, the waves were breaking high on my body, and I thought I had better go back to the beach. I made my way into shallower water. What I hadn't realised was that the knickers I was wearing had elastic in the legs. Water was filling them from the top, but was unable to get out. They ballooned out and then began to descend with the weight of the water. I was hardly able to keep my feet. I dared not let go of the break water, but tried to cling onto the offending garment with the other hand. The wind and waves were buffeting me about so much that I couldn't pull the knickers up. I managed to keep the front up, but the back slipped down, revealing my rather ample bare bottom to anyone who cared to look. At last I managed to haul myself out of the water and into my worried mother's arms. She had been watching from the beach, sure that I was going to be swept away.

I collapsed onto a towel and hurriedly dried myself off. My face burned and it wasn't just the sun! As I dressed again, my mother (relieved that I was safe) and sisters laughed until they cried. I couldn't see the joke and simply felt humiliated by the whole experience. For years afterwards I only had to hear the word 'Lowestoft' and I would blush and squirm with embarrassment. I never went there again and from that day to this, I have always hated paddling!

Seaside trips were popular, but even more so were our outings to the wonderful Wicksteed Park. This magical place was created by Charles Wicksteed, a wealthy Victorian industrialist, who purchased 100 acres of land that he opened in 1921 as a safe open, parkland for the use of local children who had nowhere else to play.

The majority of the attractions were free, which made it popular with our mothers. The downside for our mother was the fear of the dangers she felt sure would either kill or at least maim us, when we played on the free swings and slides. She was convinced we would run in front of a swing and crack our skulls open!

Wicksteed Park was close to Kettering in Northamptonshire and a comparatively short coach ride from our village, but it still seemed to take ages to get there! We would arrive mid morning and stay until six in the evening. Mum took along a packed lunch, but tea was always provided by whoever organised the outing, be it the Sunday School or the Women's Institute. It was

175

cheap day out because we spent a great deal of time riding on the free swings, slides and roundabouts, which covered a large area at the top of the park, by the café, gift shop and toilet block. A little way down were the gardens, which were beautifully kept and a quiet haven for adults to escape to when the excited shrieks of the children proved too much for them.

After the garden was the 'station' for the narrow gauge train which chugged round the perimeter of the park all day long. I think this ride cost sixpence, one of the few things that had to be paid for. The other was the Water Chute, which also cost six-pence a go.

At the bottom of the hill were the two lakes, a very shallow one that had pedal boats on it for children and a larger, deeper, more picturesque one, where adults could take out a rowing boat or punt.

There was also a rather smelly zoo, where a few depressed looking monkeys and some birds in cages were the only exhibits.

One of the best things, as far as I was concerned, that ever happened on a Wicksteed Park outing was when Mrs. Gillett fell into the boating lake!

She had to go into the rather grumpy boatman's hut, strip off and dry her clothes in front of his electric fire. It seemed Mrs. Gillett and another stalwart of the W.I. had taken out a rowing boat and half way through their allotted time had decided to change places. Poor Mrs. Gillett had missed her footing and tumbled into the murky water, which luckily, was not deep, but very smelly. Human nature being what it is, there was nothing more amusing to us than seeing this staid wife of the local Lay Preacher (and soloist at the Concert) in such an embarrassing position.

I found it even funnier because of something I over-heard a friend telling my mother. Mrs. Gillett had confided in her that her husband, in a moment of tenderness, had called her 'my roll of pink velvet'. I had visions of this soft pinkness, clad in sensible vest and knickers, huddled round the electric fire, steaming gently as she dried out after her misadventure!

My friend Gill Curtis and I once had an adventure of our own on the small lake. We had decided to take out a pedal boat. We didn't have to pay, but we were only allowed to be in a boat for an allotted time. We pedalled about for a bit then thought it would be a good idea to swap places. We pedalled the boat over to the far side of the lake and got out onto the concrete edge. This was our first mistake! The boat began to drift away from the bank. We held onto it with our hands, but we couldn't line it up enough to climb back in. Gill and I, inveterate gigglers, could see the funny side of this, and the more we giggled, the harder it became to get back into the boat. We hung on to it tightly, but no matter how we tried we just couldn't get aboard.

After a while we heard the man in charge calling out the number of our boat, announcing our time was up and we had to take the boat back to base. Panic now set in and the harder we tried, the more the boat drifted away. The man's voice became more and more strident; then after a lot of arm-waving in our direction, he came stomping over the bridge and round the lake to where we struggling with his craft.

"Your time's up." he grumbled, his face as black as thunder as he grabbed the boat from our grasp.

"We couldn't get back in the boat." We confessed sheepishly.

"Then you shouldn't have got out." he snapped. "It's not allowed."

He climbed into the boat and pedalled it across the lake, muttering,

"Stupid kids, should be old enough to know better."

We didn't go on the lake again. I know we were silly, but we didn't do any harm or damage. We simply over-ran our time and we did apologise. I have often wondered why the men employed to do jobs involving children are always so miserable. Every man in that line of work that I can remember from that era, be it cinema commissionaires, ice cream men, fair ground operators and the like, seemed, without exception, to dislike children intensely. Maybe it was a condition for the job!

After a day playing about in the park, we were ready for our tea. This was served in the café at about four o' clock and was paid for by the organisation providing the outing, funded by the various whist drives, jumble sales and the like, held throughout the year.

The Tea Rooms were on two levels. The top café served pots

of tea, dainty sandwiches and fancy cakes on delicate china at separate tables to those lucky folk who could afford the half a crown (twelve and a half pence) for the privilege, but this wasn't for the likes of Sunday School outings! We had to go into a downstairs room that catered for 'parties'.

This room had a concrete floor with rows of trestle tables covered in paper cloths and laid up with plates piled high with sandwiches (cheese, egg and cress, fish and meat paste etc.), plus cakes, far less fancy than those served upstairs, mostly things like rock buns, scones and fairy cakes. There was tea for the grown-ups and a rather weak orange squash for us children.

I longed to be able to go upstairs and select a delicious looking éclair, meringue or cream puff from the pretty tiered plates we could see through the windows, but it was never to be. "Far too extravagant!" as Mum would say!

The Vicar sometimes accompanied us on School or Sunday School outings and naturally, Miss Leppard was always on hand to flutter round him to see to his every need. What these two elderly and venerable people found to do all day at Wicksteed Park I have no idea. Certainly, they didn't ride the train, or queue up for the Water Chute; nor did they venture onto the lake. The free swings, slides and roundabouts were even less likely to appeal. I can only assume that they sat all day in the pretty gardens and discussed theology, church and school matters. Maybe they just prayed we would all get home safe and sound after the hazards of the swings and slides!

I recall the time the Vicar sat down to tea with us, sitting alongside Miss Leppard at one of the long trestle tables. After he had said Grace, he asked a waitress if he could have just plain bread and butter, rather than the sandwiches that we were all tucking into. When she brought it, we were astonished, and not a little shocked, to see him roll up half a slice of bread and butter, then dip it into his tea before eating it.

Gill and I looked at each other in amazement. If we had done the same, our mothers would have told us in no uncertain terms this was a 'disgusting habit'. Yet here was the Vicar slurping it down without anyone even mentioning it. It seemed so unfair, not that we actually wanted to dunk our bread and butter, but even so …!

Much later we found out the poor man had terminal cancer of the stomach and by dunking his food, it helped him swallow it. Naturally, Gill and I felt guilty for even noticing!

No matter where we went on these day trips, the coach always left for home at six o' clock sharp, and it was traditional to sing all the way home.

We always sang the same songs, from 'Ten Green Bottles' to 'She'll Be Coming Round The Mountain,', complete with what we thought were rather risqué words, such as "She'll be wearing pink pyjamas" and the even naughtier, "She'll be wearing Woolworth's knickers", which we considered to be hilarious and very daring indeed!

This was, to us children, the perfect way to end a 'beano' and we would arrive home tired and happy to dream of our day by the sea or in the park. Mum no doubt breathed a sigh of relief it was all over and we had come through it relatively unscathed and safe in the knowledge it would be sometime before she had to do it all again.

In the winter the great excitement was the outing to the pantomime at the Embassy Theatre in Peterborough. I loved this and was dazzled by the glitter and glamour, the dancing, the singing and music. I so envied the little girls in the children's chorus. They always wore such pretty frilly dresses and tap-shoes which clicked delightfully as they danced.

The panto was always strictly traditional, with a pretty Principal Boy, whose thigh-slapping performance in short tunic and high heels, delighted children and their fathers alike! The Dame was a man, whose grotesque 'femininity' and many changes of costume, made everyone laugh. There were also the forces for good and evil embodied in The Demon King, whom we booed and hissed at, and the Good Fairy, whom we cheered. There was also pathos, in the form of the young man whose love for the heroine was always unrequited, for instance, Buttons in Cinderella. We knew there would be a happy ending, but we still booed and cheered and hoped everything would be all right!

One year Mum, with Marion, Irene and I and her friend May Lyon, with her little son Richard, took us to the Embassy panto-

179

mime to see Cinderella, which made a change from the organised outing that was the norm. We went on the bus to Peterborough, saw the matinee performance and returned on a later bus. It was a wonderful show, colourful and filled with catchy tunes. When the show was over, we went to the toilets before leaving the theatre. As we emerged back into the auditorium, we were surprised to see the cast, still in costume, heading towards the bar at the rear of the theatre. I was amazed to see these glamorous stars, especially the young man who played Buttons. His name was Billy 'Uke' Scott and at the time was extremely popular on radio and in variety shows. He was a true star, only twenty five or so and extremely good looking, with a good singing voice and easy-going personality. He also played the ukulele-banjo, an instrument made popular by George Formby.

Billy gave us a beaming smile and came over to say hello. He asked if we'd enjoyed the show and was utterly charming and friendly. All the cast gathered round us, wanting to know where we were from and if we had travelled far to see the show. We asked if Billy would autograph our programme, which he did willingly. Mum said to me. "What a pity you don't have your autograph book here."

Billy turned to me and said. "Send it to me at the theatre, I'll sign it and get the rest of the cast to do so as well." Then with another dazzling smile, he said. "Lovely to have met you. Glad you enjoyed the show. Don't forget that autograph book now." Then he was gone.

I had admired him for sometime, but at that moment I fell head over heels in love with him and remained faithful to him until I started going to the cinema regularly and fell under the magnetic charms of Dana Andrews.

I did send Billy my autograph book and he was as good as his word, for not only did everyone of the cast sign it, but some of them stuck pictures of themselves onto the page with their signature, including Billy, who wrote "To my friend Margaret, with love from Billy 'Uke' Scott" and he added a couple of kisses for good measure. Looking back now, I think he must have been a really nice young man, who was completely unspoiled by his fame and extremely charming. That I still remember him with such warmth after more than fifty years, reinforces the power of this encounter.

He was popular for some time, but I often wonder what became of him and if he enjoyed his fame and fortune. If he is still alive today, then I hope he is well and happy. I will never forget him.

Note: Since writing this I have discovered on the internet that Billy 'Uke' Scott did indeed enjoy a successful life, helping other artistes as well as continuing to perform. At the time of writing he is living in Southport with his wife Anne and still takes to the stage occasionally, in spite of now being in his eighties.

There was another less exotic outing I recall. This was a 'one off' trip to see A Midsummer Night's Dream performed in the grounds of Hinchingbrooke Castle.

Miss Leppard walked the whole school there in an orderly crocodile from Great Stukeley on a hot summer's afternoon. The three mile walk was quite pleasant, though a little tiring when we retraced our steps in the evening. I bet we all slept well that night!

I recall very little of the play, except it looked very beautiful to my eyes. It was performed beneath a lovely old cedar tree, in front of which several fairies danced in gauzy costumes in pretty pastel shades. I remember laughing at the ludicrous Bottom with his asses head and thought Titania very glamorous indeed.

It was probably performed by the local amateur dramatic society, although it could well have been a professional touring company, which was why Miss Leppard wanted us to see it and thus receive some of the 'culture' she thought was sadly lacking from our lives.

Some of the children were bored by it, but I was entranced. I didn't understand the language, but the colourful costumes and the pretty setting compensated for this. Had it been cold and wet, then it would have lost a lot of its appeal, but the garden setting looked, smelled and sounded ravishing on that perfect summer afternoon and early evening.

That was the only time Miss Leppard took us on a trip on her own. Maybe we were too much of a handful for her to cope with single handed, or perhaps the long walk there and back was too tiring for our elderly, though energetic, teacher. Whatever the reason, we never went to see anything like it again.

These outings during the late forties and early fifties meant a great deal to the children of the village. We had few treats then, so any diversions were enjoyed to the full. Nowadays, we would be called under-privileged, but since we were all in the same boat and didn't know any different, we just got on with life and were grateful for whatever we got.

To today's children, holidays abroad are the norm, but vacations in exotic locations can't be enjoyed anymore than our annual trips to the seaside and Wicksteed Park. We loved them!

WORK

Living in a rural community during and just after the war, where many men were away in the forces, meant that there was much seasonal work to be done on the land and many village women took the opportunity to earn a little extra cash by taking on some of these jobs. The hours were fitted in for when the children were at school, or during the holidays, when we kids were expected to not only accompany our mothers, but to help with whatever job was on hand. I suspect we may have hindered them too!

My family have done many chores on the land, everything from potato picking, stooking sheaves of corn, followed by the leg-scratching agony and boredom of gleaning, potato picking, to sugar beet singling and mangold chopping. However, to my mind the most boring of these was pea-picking. As this was a comparatively light and easy job, we children were expected to help our mothers. It was sheer purgatory! We were given a basket and a sack and the idea was to fill the basket with pea pods, then transfer them to the sack and when the sack was full it was weighed by the foreman, who gave us a ticket. At the end of the day we were paid a very small sum for each ticket. It seemed to me that the sacks were huge and took forever to fill. It was usually hot and dusty in the field and work was slow as we stood next to Mum and lifted each vine, stripping off the fat green pods for what seemed like hours. I am not sure how much we were paid for each sack, but it wasn't much and so all the effort for a back-breaking day in the field reaped very little reward. It wasn't just the children who hated this job, our mothers didn't like it either. The one compensation was that we could eat a handful of delicious, fresh green peas whenever we felt like it, but the novelty of that soon wore off.

My favourite time of the farming year was harvest, mainly because for a child this could be fun as well as hard work. Adults seemed to enjoy it too and there was a carnival atmosphere in the fields as we worked.

Harvest time was always towards the end of the long school holiday, so it was nice to have something to do after weeks of idleness and boredom was about to set in. Because it was always nice weather (harvesting couldn't take place if it rained), there was a holiday feel to it and everyone seemed happy and companionable.

In the earliest days that I remember, the reaper and binder on George Gifford's farm were drawn by a couple of patient horses called Boxer and Champion. It was very rare then to see a tractor on any of the local farms until the after the war.

The horses would walk round and round the field pulling the reaper, which had great knives that cut through the wheat straw and the binder would tie it into bundles (sheaves) of a uniform size, which it threw out onto the field. The women then came along and built them into 'stooks'. This was done by picking up a sheaf under each arm and standing them head to head in groups of six or eight, making sure a gap was left running through for the air to circulate and dry out the wheat, so that the field resembled a camping ground with 'tents' made of wheat, oats or barley, or whatever cereal was being harvested that day.

These stooks were left for a day or two to dry out, then a horse and cart would come into the field with a couple of men, one of whom stood on the cart, while the other forked up the sheaves to him. It was a very skilled job to load the cart so that it was stable when stacked high.

When it was full it would be driven away to a corner of the field, where it was built into a stack, eventually to receive a sloping 'roof' and thatched, in order to make it as rain-proof as possible. My friend Jean's Dad, Jim Cox, did this thatching and always finished it off with a fancy 'corn-dolly' at each end. This was purely for decoration, but it has been said that they also warded off evil spirits.

Stooking was always the work for women and young lads, even though it was hard graft and the scratching straw made the soft skin under the arms very sore. The short, sharp stubble scratched our ankles as well, so that bathing the dust off after a day in the fields was quite painful, for our skin burned from hundreds tiny scratches. We were encouraged to wear long woollen socks to prevent this, but in very hot weather this could become unbearable, so off they would come as we took our chances with the stubble.

As I have said before, gleaning was the most boring and unrewarding job of all, for if stooking was hard work, but fun, gleaning was enough to put a child off farm work for life!

After the stooks had been cleared from the field, we would be told by our mothers to start off in a straight line from one end of the field, then walk down the rows of stubble to the other end, picking up any stalks of corn that the binder had missed. We then had to turn round and go back, until all the field had been covered. I think I am right in saying that these gleanings were a perk for the women, for they could take them home and feed the grain to their poultry. But to me, it seemed a lot of walking for very little reward, but we still had to do it, we had no choice, for as Mum would say if we complained, "You like eating the eggs, so ... " And that was that.

To the children the most exciting part of a day in the harvest field were the meal breaks, for a sandwich eaten in the open air on a hot day, was more like a picnic, even though we had to earn it by helping out. The work and the fresh air made us ravenous, so we fell upon our 'dockey' with relish.

I will take a moment here to explain the word 'dockey'. This is what farm workers called their packed lunch. The word originates from the dark days when farm workers were docked pay for any time they took off work to eat, thus the food itself became their 'dockey'.

When we were working, Mum would get up at the crack of dawn and pack our 'dockey bag' (usually a canvas haversack) with an assortment of sandwiches, that had fillings like, tomato and cheese, luncheon meat, cucumber, fish or meat paste and even jam (home made by Mum). If we were lucky there might be a piece of home made cake or a scone and maybe a few plums or cherries and an apple from our own trees. When we first went harvesting we used to take along bottles of water to slake our thirst (no fancy sodas for us then!), but this would grow tepid and unpalatable in the hot sun. We noticed that the old hands swigged constantly from bottles of cold, black tea. We tried it and found it to be very refreshing and thirst quenching, so that is what Mum made for us as well. We stacked it under the shade of a hedge along with our dockey bag to keep cool until our break. It was an acquired taste, but we learned to enjoy our special har-

187

vest drink.

All cereal crops were stooked, but some we liked and some we loathed. Wheat and oats were the best, but barley was horrible, because the awns would work their way into our clothes and irritate and scratch the skin. It was impossible to remove the little barbs and bristles from shirts and shorts, so they had to thrown away after harvest, which is why we always wore our oldest clothes. There was a crop we called 'rivet wheat' (I think that's how it is spelt), which was like barley, but shorter stemmed, with longer and sharper awns. Everyone hated this stuff, for it was vicious to handle and could rip our skin to shreds.

Harvesting was hard work (what farm work in those days wasn't?), but it was carried out in pleasant weather and the pay was quite good, if I remember rightly, for work was paid by the day, not by the 'piece', like pea-picking. It wasn't boring and there was a jolly atmosphere and the sound of laughter always present in the field.

When I was about fourteen and at school in Huntingdon, there must have been a shortage of farm workers, for there was a scheme whereby school children (over the age of thirteen, I think) were allowed time off school to help with the potato crop. I think I am right in saying that we could take off a week, but if the farmer still wanted us, then another week was allowed.

My friend Iris Turton and I applied to be allowed to go with our mothers to pick potatoes for The Pinner Brothers, Jack and Jim, who had a farm in Little Stukeley. They were known for being fair and good employers, who paid their workers well and supplied transport to and from the fields. They allowed generous time for dockey breaks and the hours were set to suit the women they employed. We would arrive at the field by nine, work until three, with a half hour break for 'breakfast' at 10am and another half hour for lunch at 12.30pm.

The regular workforce consisted of Jack, a burly, red-faced man with a bristling moustache, his good-looking, wavy haired son, Derek, who drove the tractor, which by this time had replaced the working horses, and Ellie, a young and pretty Irish girl. The rest were what they referred to as 'casual labour', part-timers like our mothers and we children.

Derek's job was to drive the tractor, which had an implement called a spinner attached to it. It spun the potatoes out of the ground and left them in neat rows for the women to pick up. Each field length was divided into measured portions called 'wretches', which were marked off with sticks. Each pair of women had to work one of these wretches, so that if they were quick, they could get their wretch picked before the spinner came round again, which gave them time for a breather, or a cigarette. At the end of each wretch stood a sack, into which the women emptied their wicker baskets full of potatoes, when the sacks were full, they were taken away and weighed. Derek got very cross if the pickers were slow and his spinner was held up for them while they finished picking their wretch. Most of the women were experienced at the job, but occasionally a new woman would be made to feel very uncomfortable, if she held up work.

Iris and I were full of enthusiasm on our first day and were allotted a wretch the same length as the women, there was no allowance made for us being complete novices at the job and children to boot. No matter how hard we worked we couldn't keep up and Derek became more and more annoyed as we held up work, for it meant he had to climb down from his tractor and help us, while the other women sat around on their upturned baskets, chatting. After a while Jack came up with the sensible idea of splitting us up and putting each of us with an experienced picker. This was a great help and we soon became more confident and capable.

My new partner was the pretty, curly haired Irish girl Ellie. She was about seventeen, with reddish-gold hair, dark blue eyes that were fringed with long dark lashes and a slow, sweet smile. She was clad in bib and brace overalls and a check shirt, that was covered by a Fair Isle cardigan and Wellington boots completed the outfit, but in spite of this unflattering garb, she still managed to look pretty and feminine.

Ellie was a full time worker at the farm and she was a wonderful partner to have, for her hands flew swiftly over the potatoes, gathering them into her basket with ease, so that it was filled in next to no time. I felt slow and clumsy by comparison, although I did improve with time.

189

It became obvious to everyone that Derek fancied Ellie and I think the feeling was mutual, because they spent their dockey breaks in each others company and they talked quietly in a secretive way, well away from everyone else. I got the idea that Jack didn't approve of this for some reason. Maybe it was because Ellie was Irish. She was one of a big family who lived in the village of Sawtry where her many big brothers had reputations for heavy drinking and fighting. I got to know her brother, John, some years later when he set up home with Doris, one of our ex-lodgers. He had the same soft Irish accent as Ellie, with the same startling blue eyes and long lashes, but he certainly didn't have Ellie's charm, and he was a very heavy drinker.

I liked Ellie a lot and enjoyed her soft, gentle voice and lilting accent. At first her conversation was shy, but she soon opened up to me and I was astonished at her tales of life with her rowdy, drunken family, which was so unlike my own home.

Although Ellie talked to me and to Derek, she had little to do with the other women. I presume since she was a lot younger than them, they had little in common with her, for she was a young single girl and they were all mature married women.

After our first day in the potato field we climbed wearily into the lorry at three o clock. I was exhausted and almost fell asleep on the short journey home. After I'd cleaned up I slumped into a chair, too tired to do anything. My back and thighs ached, my hands were rough and raw and I didn't have the strength to do anything but sleep. I had never worked so hard in all my life, but I had really enjoyed myself and felt a great deal of satisfaction, for I had earned the enormous sum of ten shillings (50p), which seemed like a fortune to me. The women were paid a magnificent seventeen shillings and sixpence a day, which was really excellent pay at that time.

If it rained it made 'spud picking' impossible, because if the ground was water-logged and sticky the spinner couldn't get the potatoes out, but if it was just a shower, we could get into a barn and wait for it to pass. This was great fun for us youngsters, for we could climb on the bales of hay, or enjoy an unscheduled dockey break. It the rain was persistent, then we had to be found other jobs, or be sent home, which meant no pay, of course.

One day when it was particularly wet we were taken to a field to chop mangold worzels. These huge root vegetables, which looked a little like turnips, only much bigger, were used for cattle food. I recall thinking how beautiful they were, for they came in a range of colours from pale pink to deep purple.

We were given a large curved knife, then Jack showed us how to pick up the mangold by its tough leaves in our left hand, then chop off the root with the knife in our right hand. The leaves were discarded and the roots flung into the back of a cart to be trundled off to the barn for storage. It was a highly dangerous job for anyone, let alone children and it is a miracle that we didn't manage to chop off a few fingers along with the leaves! I don't think children would be allowed to use such sharp and danger-ous implements today, just the thought of it would send the Health and Safety Inspector rushing round to stop it! However, we didn't come to any harm.

We liked picking potatoes on the rich black fenland best of all, for it drained well and didn't stick to the crop or boots as we worked, like the sticky clay in some of the fields on the farm.

Another job we had to do when it rained was carrot pulling. This was tedious and back breaking work and very fiddly too, for we had to pull the carrots from the ground, count them, bundle up them into neat bunches and tie them with a length of raffia. Ellie was brilliant at this and soon amassed many neat bundles in her basket. My bunches were fewer, untidy and messy, so I was full of admiration at her expertise.

After a field of potatoes had been picked we were each given a basket by Jack and assembled into a row at the headland of the field, then at a given signal we had to walk from one end to the other picking up any potatoes that had been missed "Pick 'em all up!" Yelled Jack. "Even the doll's eyes." From that day on, my mother and I always called tiny new potatoes, 'doll's eyes'!

Gleaning a potato field was as hated and as boring as glean-ing after a cereal crop, we walked miles for very little reward. I think it was an insurance that the field would not have potatoes growing up in between whatever crop was next scheduled for it.

Iris and I worked for the Pinner Brothers for a couple of weeks at least that autumn. I earned two pound ten shillings a week and bought myself a pair of shoes, which was a great help to mum and made me very proud to do it. I think I managed to get myself a new drawing book and some pencils as well, which was a great luxury and a joy for me.

If potato picking was profitable work for kids, then there were plenty of jobs that paid pennies rather than pounds.

Just after the war there was a plague of cabbage white butterflies, whose caterpillars decimated the cabbages in fields and gardens, so school children were paid to kill them. Extraordinary to think of it now, but I suppose in those days insecticides weren't as readily available as they are today, so they paid us a penny for a hundred Cabbage White corpses. We would set off after school armed with nothing more than a empty jam jar. The field behind our house was a good hunting ground, for it seemed to have clouds of the pretty white insects fluttering about over whatever crop was there. We would soon capture them in our hands, then deftly pull off their heads and drop the still moving body into the jar. When the jar was full, we would take it to school, where Miss Leppard would count the by now rather smelly corpses and give us a penny for every hundred that we supplied. I have no idea what she did with them. Looking back now, I don't know how we could have done such a thing, but we didn't turn a hair and became quite expert at catching the butterflies.

Dad would also get us to walk round his cabbage patch with a jam jar full of salt water, into which we dropped any caterpillars that we found. We didn't get paid for this, but we were expected to do it in order to keep our supply of cabbages, broccoli or Brussels sprouts pest free. It makes me shudder to think of doing these things now, but it was all part of surviving during those difficult days, so if there was something that the children could do to help, then that is what we had to do.

I am told that farm workers could make a little 'beer money' by catching rats, for which they would be paid a shilling (5p) for every tail they supplied as proof of killing the offending rodent. Children weren't encouraged to go after this game, as hunting and killing a rat was far too specialised and dangerous a job for them. I don't think I could have done that anyway. Killing an insect was one thing, but dispatching a warm blooded creature, even if it is considered vermin, was quite another matter.

A far more pleasant job, though hardy well paid, was collecting rose hips in the autumn. It had just been discovered that rose hip syrup was a good source of vitamins, so they paid school children to collect them from the hedgerows, where the wild roses that had bloomed in June had produced the scarlet hips that hung like jewels and glowed in the autumn sunshine.

It was pleasant enough to wander round the fields, picking the brightly coloured fruits, putting them into baskets and eventually taking vast quantities to school to be weighed by Miss Leppard or Miss Smith. I can't recall precisely what we were paid, but I think it was something like a penny a pound, which was hardly generous, when one considers the amount of work (and scratched arms and legs from the briars) that we had to put in, but at least we did get to sample the fruits of our labours, for one day Miss Leppard showed us a large bottle of the sweet, pale pink liquid that smelled of roses.

"This is what the rose hips you have picked have been turned into." She announced. "Now form a line, eldest at the front and you can have a spoonful to try."

We did as we were bid and Miss Leppard stood at the head of the queue with the bottle in one hand and a teaspoon in the other. Each child stepped forward in turn, mouth open to receive their first ever taste of Rose Hip Syrup. It tasted OK, sweet, sticky and scented, but it wasn't all that wonderful. We all took the stuff from the same spoon, which wasn't wiped between each dose, so we no doubt took in a few of our school chums germs along with the syrup!

Not that this worried us in the least, for we would often share a 'gobstopper' with a friend. These huge sweets changed colour as layer after layer of sugar was sucked off, so we'd say in response to their request, "Give us a suck of your gobstopper."

"Okay, but only until it changes colour." Which meant that grubby fingers were used to take it out of the mouth to inspect it. Ugh! Worse still, was letting someone have a chew of your chewing gum! Quite disgusting, but we never came to any harm from these horrible practices!

There was also a scheme, similar to the rose hip one, when we were asked to pick up acorns and take them to school where they were to be collected by farmers and used for pig food, I believe. However, I didn't know of any oak trees close to my home, so I didn't join in that scheme.

Salvage, was another important word in our vocabulary during the war. Today it is called 're-cycling'.

There was a scheme run by the schools that encouraged children to collect books, magazines, newspapers and cardboard. There was no money in this, it was simply our patriotic duty and our contribution to 'the war effort'. However, there was an incentive to make us strive to collect more paper than our school friends.

All the paper collected was weighed and depending on how much there was, a child was given a ranking. For instance, the initial collection, a child would be given the rank of 'Private', with a badge to pin onto one's lapel. The ranks rose with each collection, until one could reach the dizzy heights of 'Field Marshal', but this was after weeks of graft.

I can't remember what rank I reached, but 'Adjutant' rings a bell.

There were excellent perks to be gained from this scheme, even though there was no pay. For after we collected books, magazines, comics and even hard backed books from friends and neighbours, we took them home to sort them and everyone took the opportunity to browse through everything before it was taken to school to be weighted. Our family budget didn't run to magazines, so all the family loved looking through the wonderful Picture Post and a small, but thick little book called Lilliput, which had tastefully posed 'art studies' of naked ladies. I used to call these rude books, but Dad liked them! There were also lots of American comics and film magazines given to families by their G.I. friends and it was these that I loved. In fact, all the family found something of interest to read before it was all bundled up and taken to school for collection for re-cycling. I will admit here that I did succumb to temptation and kept any hard backed books that took my fancy, but I don't feel too guilty about it. I don't think the 'war effort' suffered too much from my creaming off some of the donations, for it was small enough reward for what was really quite hard work for children.

All these schemes made us realise that 'out there' a war was being fought but I am pleased to say that the horrors of it never came to close to home, which is quite surprising since we were surrounded by air fields, so it was a miracle that we weren't the target for more bombing raids. The only bombs I can remember falling on the village were a few incendiary bombs that fell in the Park, without damaging any property, thank goodness.

Some people may think it wrong , or even cruel to make children work the way we were encouraged to do, but I am sure it helped us realise that if we wanted something, then we had to earn it, thus teaching us the value of money.

During the war and soon after, there was a shortage of men to do many jobs, so women took over and luckily, with land work, children could be taken along. Many a mother worked with her baby in a pram beside her and the children who were old enough were expected to help with some of the less arduous tasks, every little helped!

Mostly, I enjoyed the jobs I did when I was a child, some were more pleasant than others, but on the whole they were fun and I don't regret for one minute having to help out.

THE VILLAGE HOP

The W.I. Hall (also known as the W.I. Hut) was the scene of many exciting events during my early years, but none was more thrilling to me than the monthly Saturday night dances that were held throughout the autumn and winter.

I was about eleven when I was first allowed to accompany my mother to one of these. She, as a W.I. member, used to go along to help with the refreshments, for tea, sandwiches and cakes were served in the interval We always arrived fairly early, for my friend Gill's mother, Mrs. Curtis , was the caretaker and she, with the help of Mum and my friend Iris's mother, Mrs. Turton, liked to get the urns on and the tea cups and saucers set out before the crowds arrived.

The door opened to the public around 7.30-8pm and proceedings were brought to a halt promptly at midnight, for there was a rule (or possibly a law) forbidding dancing on the Sabbath. Refreshments (no alcohol) were served around 10pm.

Whilst the ladies made sandwiches and sorted out the rest of the food and drinks in the little kitchen, Gill, Iris and I would be told to sprinkle the floor boards with French chalk, bought specially for the purpose, for this made the floor slippery and dancing was easier . I recall once when we were too liberal with this and the results were a floor as slick and slippery as an ice rink, making it almost impossible for couples to keep on their feet!

Music for dancing was supplied by Sid King and his Music. Sid was not a musician, however, for his 'music' was made by way of records of popular dance orchestras, like Victor Sylvester, Joe Loss and Stanley Black, as well as American bands like Glenn Miller and the like, which he played on a turntable with amplifiers to fill the hall with music. He was, I suppose, the forerunner of the disco.

Sid King was a lorry driver from the village of Ellington. He was tallish, with black wavy hair, thick lensed horn-rimmed spectacles and a ruddy complexion. He was assisted by a young man we only knew as Birdie. He wore his fair hair slicked back with Brylcreem, was about the same height as Sid and had the red-faced look of an outdoor worker, which he was, for Birdie was a farm worker.

Gill, Iris and I regarded Sid and Birdie as sort of 'showbiz' personalities, for these latter-day disc jockeys hosted the proceedings with much panache and expertise. They would announce through the microphone what the next dance would be and urged everyone to " ... take your partners ..." for a quick step, fox trot or waltz. They would sometimes add a witty remark or two to cover any gaps between records. We thought them very glamorous! Sid especially had the ability to make me giggle, because he had a way of making what I thought was an hilarious remark with a perfectly straight face, which I found very funny indeed.

Until the Three Horseshoes closed at 10pm, the hall would be almost empty, which was good for Gill, Iris and I, for it meant we had room to practice our dancing with each other and also with our mothers, who also danced together in between making sandwiches. There may have been the odd father there, but I am sure it was exclusively women and kids like us.

My Dad was never there, because he had to be at home baby-sitting my sisters, which is why Mum took me along. It was company for her to have me to walk home with after the dance.

Both Sid and Birdie were excellent dancers and gave us lots of useful lessons on the more intricate steps and how to make fancy moves at the corners of the hall. I remember him showing us how to do the samba, which we thought was very exotic! This was all valuable stuff and stood me in good stead when I was a teenager and dancing became the most important thing in my life.

It was at these village hops that I learned how to dance and came to know the joy of moving to music. Later on, during our carefree teenage years, Iris and I would cycle for miles to go to a dance if there wasn't one near at hand. We have set off in rain, hail and snow to get to a venue, but mostly we went to the dances that were held each Saturday in the Town Hall in Huntingdon, where we spent a half a crown (twelve and a half pence) of our hard earned money to dance to local bands like Reg Farminer (who worked in a local grocery shop) and George Green (who was an undertaker). Occasionally, we would be asked to pay the princely sum of three and sixpence when the famous Blue Diamonds from the University Arms Hotel were on the bill. We thought they were worth every penny of this exorbitant entrance fee!

However, that was all to come. In the meantime, it was at the village hops that we honed our skills and the most important lesson we learned was how to follow ones partner. This was essential, for if any of the men, mellow from their pint or two of ale, asked us to dance, then because they were unsteady on their feet, it took a lot of agility to prevent our toes getting crushed. I became so nimble, that I was often asked later on in life, if I had had dancing lessons!

Around ten fifteen people began to arrive in dribs and drabs. There were always several couples who made a noisy entrance after spending a good nights drinking at the Three Horseshoes. This group was led by a couple of local farming brothers and their friends. They were loud and jolly, laughing loudly as they swung themselves around the hall with gay abandon.

Soon the hall was crowded with couples, married , engaged or simply courting, plus a few single boys and girls who were hoping to dance with the people they fancied and trying to avoid those they didn't.

The men who asked kids of our age to dance, were usually the fathers of friends, or maybe an older brother, mellow with beer, might take pity on us and circumnavigate the floor with us until they saw someone more interesting to partner. However, I don't recall any lads of our age at dances, for they seemed to think (unlike today's youth) that dancing was 'sissy', until the attraction of the opposite sex made them realise that dancing was a golden opportunity not only to meet girls, but to hold them close for the duration of a dance.

We didn't mind at all about the lack of boys at that time, for we just enjoyed dancing for its own sake. We weren't looking for romance, so were happy to dance with each other.

Gill and I enjoyed a fast and furious (and if I may say, extremely skilful) polka, which was always included in the selection of Old Tyme, sequence and Novelty Dances, that were always a highlight of village hops.

Iris and I favoured the ballroom dances, like the waltz and foxtrot, although I think the quickstep was our favourite. We also liked the exotic tango, rumba and samba, although our version was much less flamboyant than the versions we later saw on TVs 'Come Dancing'!

During the last part of the evening, after the refreshments had been served, Sid and Birdie would take it in turns to play records, while the other danced. It was during this time that the Novelty Dances were so popular that great lines of people would link up and leap about doing the Palaise Glide to tunes like 'Horsey, horsey, don't you stop.' or 'Ten Little Girls From The Village School.' and performing the boisterous 'Hokey Cokey', when the dancers were often far too enthusiastic in throwing their 'left legs in and out' on the rickety wooden floor, that the needle would skip a groove on the record and Sid or Birdie would have to dash over and set it right.

By eleven o clock the little hall would become so hot and smoky that we would go and stand by the door to cool down and gulp in some fresh air. We didn't stray further than the door, because it could be embarrassing to go right outside, for we might bump into a courting couple having a kiss and cuddle in the friendly shadows of the bicycle shed.

Gill and I were once got shouted at for peering at a couple doing just that from the tiny window in the ladies loo!

At around 11.50pm Sid would ask everyone to "Take your partners for the last waltz.", the lights would then be dimmed and couples would take the floor for the last dance of the evening. It was tradition that the last waltz was danced with the one who was special to you, or maybe someone who would ask to 'walk you home'. This was all very romantic and could be exciting if the one you fancied asked you to dance with them, but it could be equally heart breaking if he asked someone else.

The tune for this last waltz was always the smooch 'Whose Taking You Home Tonight?'. When this ended Sid put on a record of the National Anthem, during which everyone stood to attention, then that was it , it was all over and we poured into the cloakroom to retrieve our coats, then after making sure that everyone had gone and the hall was empty, Mrs. Curtis would lock up. We then said our goodbyes and Mum and I wended our weary way home along the lane . It was about 12.30am by the time we got in. Dad and the twins would be fast asleep in bed.

I was always exhausted by the time we got home, but even though my feet ached and I couldn't wait to get into bed, I would fall asleep thinking that our village hops were the best in the world and I couldn't wait for the four weeks to pass so that we could do it all over again.

FOOD AND RATIONING

I believe that living in the country was an advantage during the war, because apart from the lack of bombing, life was easier because we could obtain free food. It had to worked for, but the effort was worth it.

For instance, the field next to our house grew an abundance of horse radish plants, so occasionally, at Mum's suggestion, we would take a trowel and dig out the roots for her to process into a piquant sauce to accompany our roast beef. Horse radish roots are really long and grow deep into the ground, so digging them up was very hard work indeed, for the leaves were tough and scratchy and the over-powering odour of the roots clung to our hands for days. Mum would clean the roots, Dad would grate them and the pulp was made into a creamy sauce, that she stored in little jars. I think she added other ingredients, but I have no idea what it was. The resulting product was fiery and tasty. My Dad loved it. I did when I was older, but as a child it was far too strong a flavour for my taste.

Grating the roots was an eye-watering job, even worse than peeling onions and shallots for pickling, so Dad (whose job it was to do these chores) would wear his gas mask, we would follow suit as the odour penetrated our noses and set our eyes watering. It was an hilarious sight to see us sitting around in our gas masks while Dad did this job, because whoever was in the vicinity suffered and wearing our gas masks really did help.

We were supposed to carry our gas masks with us wherever we went and we did at first, but after a while we became very cavalier in our attitude toward them and we only carried them to school on days when we knew the man would be there to inspect them to make sure they fitted correctly. I hated even trying mine on, for the black rubber was smelly and the greeny-blue metallic disc with holes in it, made the whole thing look grotesque. It also felt very claustrophobic. The little children had red Mickey Mouse type gas masks, with round black ears. I think these looked even more horrible than the ordinary black ones, although the idea was to make them more acceptable to young kids. There was also a large black contraption, into which a baby could be laid. It had a pump affair at the side for the parent to ventilate the baby inside. It makes me shudder to think how terrible it must have been to have to use these gas masks in a real 'gas alert' situation. Luckily, we only used ours as protection from the strong odour of peeled onions and horse radish!

Mushrooms were a seasonal delicacy that we all enjoyed. Early mornings in late summer and autumn were the best times for collecting these and there is no more satisfying a job than walking over a field (in our case, the Park) on a fine morning and returning with a basketful of the delicious delicate flavoured fungi. Our favourites were the big, flat white ones that had dark, almost black gills. The smell of these frying or stewing gently in their own juice was mouth-watering. No commercially grown mushroom taste half as good as those we picked fresh from the fields. I am sure that they are still available today, if one knows where to look.

Blackberries, too, were a useful addition to our menus and these, stewed with apples from our own trees, or made into a delicious pie, pudding or crumble, was a treat indeed.

My Dad loved to set off on a late summer afternoon, our dog Trixie, at his heels, to pick basketsful of the lush dark fruits.

My friend Jean Cox and I also knew where to find the best blackberries and would take a bowl or basket, a stick to reach down the topmost brambles and walk across to Lord Dees, the field that had the best and largest berries. Since this field was rather remote, it wasn't over-picked by others, so we usually had first choice. We would help ourselves to handfuls of the ripe, juicy fruit and cram them into our mouths, unwashed, not worrying at all about dust and flies. Along the side of the lane grew another sort of fruit, closely related to the blackberry, that we called dewberries. They were rounder, looser in texture, with less of the tiny seeds that blackberries had. They were delicious to eat raw, but because they were less firm, they would turn to a mushy pulp if stewed.

Children had all kind of delicacies that we liked to eat and although we swore they tasted good, some of them were downright horrible!

For instance, we have been known to try and eat sloes, which is the fruit of the blackthorn. These tiny black fruits, with a hard stone at its centre, looked a little like damsons, but that is where the similarity ended, for sloes were so sour that they made the inside of one's mouth pucker and dry up. The only thing a sloe is good for, is making gin, but that wasn't an option in our house, because we didn't have access to the gin that is needed to make the stuff.

The flesh of the rose hip is quite pleasant to taste, but nibbling the flesh is fraught with danger, because the fine hairs that cover the seeds inside are likely to work their ways into lips and tongue and this causes great irritation, which is not surprising, since boys, who thought it was a highly amusing practical joke, made an itching powder with these hairs as one of the ingredients. So after eating one rose hip and having to try and get the fine hairs out of a lip, if one was sensible one never tried it again. It was just misery.

We did try eating the fruit of the hawthorn, for the crimson coloured haws looked so inviting, but the flesh was mushy and rather bland, so we left them for the birds! The emerging new leaves of the same tree were also eaten by some children and called 'bread and cheese', although why this was the case I have no idea. I did try it (naturally), but disliked both taste and texture and never tried it again.

Crab apples look wonderful and there were plenty of trees around, but their glowing red/yellow fruits didn't taste as good as they looked, for they were almost as sour as the sloes, however, we would take them home and Mum would transform them into a delicious, pale pink jelly, with a rich apple flavour all its own, so once again we had free (almost) food.

Sucking on a cowslip, oxlip or primrose flower gave one a tantalisingly tiny sip of sweetness, but a whole field full wouldn't have satisfied the taste buds of children deprived as we were of sweets and chocolate bars. Some village women would turn these flowers into wine, but my mother wasn't one of them. She wasn't interested in making alcohol, food was her prime concern, although Dad did have a go at wine making in his later years, but most of it was too sweet and sticky for my taste.

'Digging For Victory' was a phrase familiar to everyone in wartime and just about every mansion, house, cottage, country estate and public park turned most, if not all, their land into space to grow vegetables. Not only was this helping 'the war effort' by making us as self sufficient as possible, but it was cheaper than having to buy produce from the shops.

Dad was a competent gardener, who grew a good range of vegetables for the table. He grew potatoes, both early and main crop, carrots, onions, cabbages, broccoli, runner, broad and French beans, marrows and lots of salad vegetables. We children were encouraged to grow easy things like radishes and it was very exciting to grow a crop of mustard and cress, by sprinkling the seed onto a flannel placed over a saucer of water. This grew rapidly and we were soon able to harvest our crop and there was nothing as sweet as making a sandwich with the mustard and cress we grew ourselves. Add chopped boiled egg and you have a feast fit for a king!

Any surplus fruit and vegetables, whether from the garden or the hedgerows, Mum would bottle, pickle or make jam with. All fruits like plums, damsons, greengages and blackberries were packed into Kilner jars, which she treated in a way that preserved them. I thought these glass jars of fruits looked beautiful, with their jewel-like colours, when she stored them on the larder shelf.

Apples were peeled and cored and sliced into rings and dried. They were then packed into air tight tins until required, when she would soak them and they would be magically restored to their original texture. There may have been more to this process, but I can't remember it, if there was.

Surplus runner beans were sliced and packed into a large earthenware crock, with layers of salt in-between the layers of beans, finishing with a salt layer. Naturally, when these were used, they had to soaked for a long time to rid them of the salt. I seem to remember that they tasted very good and certainly better than tinned runner beans, which personally, I think are disgusting!

Although we had pet rabbits, we didn't ever intend that they should be used for the pot, but Mum wasn't averse to accepting a wild rabbit from a friendly farm worker or neighbour who hunted them with ferrets, or caught them in traps and she gratefully turned these into a delicious stew, or even better, a pie. Occasionally a hare would come our way, although the strong taste was really too 'gamey' for us children, but she never turned down any that were offered, for it all helped to eke out the meat ration.

Rabbit was a popular meal for country folk for many years, for they were plentiful and easy to catch, especially if you had ferrets and I believe farmers were more tolerant of people taking rabbits from their land, as this helped to cull them when they became a pest and ate their crops. Then the terrible disease myxamatosis was introduced in the 1950s, in order to rid the countryside of what had become a pest.

It was a harrowing sight to see these poor infected animals, blind, with terrible lesions and sores, just sitting waiting to die by the side of the lane, in fields and even our gardens. Many a farm worker was upset and horrified by this cruel disease and took to carrying a stout stick with them when they walked on the land, so they could dispatch the poor creatures as humanely as possible when they came across them.

We never ate rabbit again, nor did 99% of the people who had once enjoyed it. Although we all knew that the disease couldn't cross from rabbit to humans, we just didn't fancy it.

Ironically, the rabbits that did survive, developed an immunity to the disease and thrived, so that nowadays there are just as many as there were before. Hopefully, no one will ever use such a cruel and devastating disease to cull animals again. Many of the brutal traps that were used are now illegal, thank goodness.

We did keep chickens and ducks for eggs, but as I have already explained, we were all far too soft hearted and sentimental about them to want to eat them.

Our hens had a nice, large well-appointed run with a shed that contained several nesting boxes, lined with fresh, sweet hay. Did our hens lay their eggs in them? Of course not! They preferred to lay them in a clump of nettles, or in a pile of dusty grass clippings, in fact, anywhere other than the place that had been provided for them, especially, somewhere as inaccessible as possible! Once their laying days were over, these fat and pampered fowl, spent their retirement, along with their more productive sisters, in luxury, scratching contentedly at the ground and living on the best quality scraps and a disgusting smelling ingredient that they loved. My mother called this 'mash' and she mixed it in with their boiled up vegetable peeling etc. I hated it when this big old iron pot was bubbling away. The smell made me retch, but the hens adored it.

I remember something that was a great mystery to me when I was very young. If we had a broody hen (one that sat all day on her nesting box, clucking maternally), Mum would say that she would have to buy a clutch of eggs for her to sit on, in order for us to have some baby chicks to rear. I was curious as to why she couldn't sit on our own hen's eggs. It seemed silly that Mum had to buy some from a neighbour when we had perfectly good eggs of our own.

"Why can't she sit on our eggs? I asked.

"They wouldn't hatch." Mum said.

"Why?"

"Because we haven't got a cockerel, so we have to buy eggs from someone who has."

This seemed extremely puzzling to me, because everyone knew that cockerels didn't lay eggs, so why on earth did it matter that we didn't have one.

When questioned further, Mum said " Eggs aren't fertile unless there's a cockerel in the hen coop." And that was the end of the conversation!

All in all, I think our hens must have been the most pampered birds in the village, for they lived to a ripe old age, growing fat on the exotic scraps they received, courtesy of the Officers Mess at The Hall!

If one of our hens was off colour, Mum would put it in a box and bring it in to recuperate in peace away from the noise and bustle of the hen run. She would set its box by the fire in the kitchen, hand feed it and it was not unknown for her to add a drop of brandy to the milk she spooned down its throat, this from the precious little bottle that she kept by her for 'medicinal purposes'.

One such sick hen spent a few nights mollycoddled like this, then the next day, when it was obvious that she was well again, Mum took her out and returned her to the hen run. That night, I heard a tapping at the door and went to open it, but was surprised to see nobody there. Then I heard a contented clucking, looked down and saw the hen that had been ill. She strutted past me, went into the kitchen and settled herself down, preening and clucking contentedly as she prepared to spend another night by the fire! It was very funny and we all laughed, but Mum was firm and an indignant Mrs. Chicken was returned to her own quarters alongside her less pampered sisters.

I loved it when a clutch of eggs hatched. There is no more enchanting sight than seeing a mother hen scratching in the dust, surrounded by a batch of yellow balls of fluff. However, it was a rather haphazard way of replenishing laying birds, for no one knew how many chicks would be pullets (young females) or cockerels, so a better and more reliable way was to buy day old chicks that had been sexed. Unfortunately, the adorable yellow fluffy stage didn't last long and within weeks the babies had turned into ugly, leggy, squawking adolescents, without an ounce of charm. But it wasn't long before they were laying lovely brown eggs for us, so we forgave them their unattractiveness.

Collecting eggs must be one of the most pleasant job a child can do. I used to love taking a bowl and putting my hand into a warm nest, to feel the smooth shell of the egg as I lifted it out and placed it carefully into my bowl. Any child who hasn't done this should be considered deprived, for it is one of the joys of living in the country. Then the enjoyment of eating a boiled egg that you have collected yourself for breakfast or tea, is such a pleasure. Dipping a bread and butter, or toast, 'soldier' into the rich, deep yellow yolk of a free range egg you have gathered yourself, is something very special. Luckily, I still get my eggs from a lady who raises her chickens with care and consideration, so I can enjoy my breakfast egg just the same. The only thing missing, is collecting it myself!

When we were very small, at Easter time, Mum would colour the eggs, blue (with ink), pink (with cochineal) yellow (boiled with onion skin) and some even had pretty patterns. These would be in our hens nesting boxes when we collected the eggs on Easter Day. We were astonished and full of wonder that not only did our hens know it was Easter, so they could lay their pretty eggs for us, but that they also managed to lay hard boiled eggs as well!

When I was older I was allowed to assist Mum in making these magical Easter eggs and I am sure no elaborate chocolate egg, wrapped in fancy silver paper and ribbon, could give more pleasure than those 'special' eggs from our own hens laid all those years ago gave to us.

The few Khaki Campbell ducks Mum kept were prolific layers and since we also had a drake, if one of our hens became broody, then she might put a few under her. Ducks, for some reason, are not good mothers, at least ours weren't, so it was not unusual to see a motherly brown hen clucking over a brood of adorable, fluffy, yellow ducklings.

Duck eggs are excellent for cooking, although the flavour is sometimes considered too strong for boiling or frying. I liked them and enjoyed the sight of the deep orangey-yellow yolks that contrasted with the translucent, bluish white. I was, however, always disappointed that our ducks laid eggs that were white and not that pretty, greenish-blue colour one associates with duck eggs. These ducks, like our hens, lived in a sort of duck heaven until death claimed them and they were given a dignified burial, before they winged their way to that great poultry coop in the sky.

I have a vague memory of Mum once making a rook pie. She must have been desperate, for this wasn't something that she would normally set before us and I doubt she told us what was in the pie until we'd eaten it! I think the pie must have been mainly vegetables and pastry anyway, because there isn't a lot of flesh on a rook!

Looking back now to those far off days of rationing, which didn't end until 1953 and became even worse after the war ended, I wonder that my poor mother didn't collapse from sheer exhaustion, for throughout the war years she had no electricity at all in the house, so there were no labour saving devices like a vacuum cleaner, dish washer or washing machine and certainly no refrigerator , nor was she to have one for many years. After the war, the Estate Managers saw fit to install electricity to its tenants houses, but for some reason, this was only for downstairs, we still needed candles or lamps to see our way to bed.

The war years saw her cooking, washing, cleaning and generally looking after a husband, three children, evacuees, lodgers and a succession of cats, dogs, pet mice, rabbits, ducks and chickens, who all helped to mess up the house she spent hours cleaning, yet she still found the energy to do the laundry for a couple of G.I.s, as well as working on the land from time to time. In between all this she found time to make jam, bottle fruit, make pickles, chutneys and relishes and preserve any surplus produce from the garden. Nothing was wasted and if something could be kept for future use, then Mum found a way to do it. We often used to say that during the bottling and jam making season, if we didn't keep moving, we would find ourselves topped and tailed and bottled before you could say " Knife!"

Our favourite was her jam. During the most stringent rationing, women were allowed to forgo their jam ration and take extra sugar instead, which thank goodness, Mum did, for her plum or greengage jam, or the delicious pale pink crab apple jelly were far superior to the shop bought stuff. The smell of the house on jam-making days was wonderful. She would boil up the fruit and sugar concoction, then drop small amounts onto a saucer to see if there was a 'good set'. This was ensured once the little blob on the saucer wrinkled when lightly pushed with a finger. Bread wasn't rationed (only for a short while after the war), so we could look forward to a teatime after school when we would probably have a boiled egg with bread and butter (or margarine) 'soldiers', followed by delicious bread and jam, or maybe a home made scone or two. Nowadays, of course, most people have a cooked meal in the evening, but not then.

Wartime was very hard for some people, I know, but for us it wasn't so bad. We lived in comparative safety in a country village, Dad was a good and methodical gardener, who strived to provide his family with a quantity of fresh vegetables, plus a few flowers for pleasure and Mum was a first class cook and could turn her hand to making a meal out of anything … or practically nothing! She didn't go in for fancy stuff, but her pastry was as light as a feather, her cakes were mouth-wateringly delicious; her casseroles, roasts and other meat dishes, were as nourishing as they were appetizing. We sometimes took a packed lunch to school, but mostly we came home for lunch and there was always a hot meal, plus a pudding, waiting for us.

Rationing or not, I can never remember having to go without a good meal, although looking back, I recall that sometimes Mum didn't eat with us, assuring us that she wasn't hungry.

How, I wonder, would I and my contemporaries, be able to manage with strict rationing today. One egg per person per week, two ounces of butter and so on. Even after the war I can remember that meat rationing became even more stringent. My late husband, who was a butcher, said that at one time in the late 1940s each person was allowed to have eight pennyworth of meat per week (that's less than 4 pence in today's currency), plus two pennyworth of corned beef. The government imported all kinds of things to help eke out our meat ration. Snoek (pronounced 'snook') a South African fish was one such item and we were all persuaded that whale meat was delicious. Neither of these food items caught on. I think people preferred to go without rather than eat, what was by all accounts, quite disgusting!

Luckily, during the war years the staples like bread, potatoes and I think I am right in saying flour, were not rationed, so we could fill up on these things. I loved bread (and still do), so it was no hardship for me to have a sandwich!

When rationing did finally end, we thought we would be living once again in a land of plenty, but I remember that immediately sweets were taken off the ration, the shops were empty and we all bemoaned the fact that at least with our allocation of a quarter of a pound a week, we had some sweets to enjoy, but now we had none at all. They even rationed potatoes for a while, but it was farce, because there were always plenty for everyone. One of the good things about sweet rationing, although we didn't appreciate it at the time, was the fact that it was good for our teeth. I, at the age of 68, have only one tooth missing and I lost that to an alcoholic school dentist! That my dental health is so good must be due to the lack of sugary drinks, sweets and chocolate in my childhood.

We are told that during the war the food experts devised a diet that was healthy and inexpensive. It may have been, but it was also dull and without the variety of goods that we can buy everyday now. My family, like many others in the village, were lucky to have parents who worked hard to give us the best that they could in difficult circumstances and for that I am very grateful indeed.

GAMES

Me and playmate Pam Jones

Until the advent of electronic games machines, I don't think children's games had changed a great deal over the years, except for a few regional differences and I expect a few of the more ancient forms have been updated, but basically, they have remained the same for generations.

When I was very little a great favourite was a singing game called 'The Farmer's In His Den', which is still enjoyed by young children today.

Another similar game was 'Poor Jenny Is A-weeping', which little girls loved to play. I was surprised when my sister-in-law, Eileen, told me that she knew this as 'Poor Mary is A-weeping', which I thought was an interesting variation, considering our villages were barely three miles apart.

There were many such games that were accompanied by songs or chants. I seem to remember that these were strictly playground games and not often played out of the school environment.

A great favourite at our village school was Sticky Toffee, but we called it Press, which probably got its name from Press Gang, for it entailed the person who was 'It' catching another, then joining hands, to chase another, who added to the chain, until there was a long line of children wheeling across the playground to catch the few that had so far escaped. The last person to be caught was then 'It' and the game began again. I remember that being on the end of a long line of children running and wheeling across the steeply sloping tar and gravel playground could be exhilarating, but hazardous, for the momentum that built up was considerable and it was sometimes hard to keep ones feet and many a knee and elbow was scraped whilst playing Press, so it could be dangerous, especially if one was flung against the wall of the school, although I don't recall any injuries other than the odd graze or bruise.

These catching games were very popular and there were many variations on a theme. There was 'Tiggy, Tiggy, touch!', which before play began, whoever was 'It' decided that touching something would make one immune from being caught. This could be a colour, a material, or a piece of the playground. A variation was 'Tiggy Off The Ground', which meant immunity was gained by getting ones feet off the ground in some way.

The very little children liked to play 'The Big Ship Sails Through The Alley, Alley-oo.' This was played by the first child in a line placing his hand against a wall, while the other joined hands and passed through the gap between arm and wall, singing,

'The big ship sails through the Alley, alley-oo,
The alley, alley-oo, the alley, alley-oo,
The big ships sails through the alley, alley-oo,
On the last day of September.'

This was repeated over and over again until all the children had passed beneath another child's arms and they all faced the same way with their arms crossed in front of them. When the last child was through, they sang it all over again and unwound until they were free and back to the child who was against the wall. This was fun for the tiny tots, but became boring as one got older. My friend, Megan, who is six at the time of writing, tells me that this is still played by children today.

These games for the infants were played by both boys and girls, but as we got older, so the sexes separated and boys played one set of games and the girls another.

For instance, boys would never be seen skipping, or throwing a ball against the wall, as girls did, but they liked to kick a ball about, or play French Cricket, or a variation on that that we called Hot Rice, all of which was very competitive and entailed a lot of hard tackling. Boys also played marbles and war games, but the girls never joined in. No one said we couldn't, it was simply an unwritten law.

The ball games the girls played were often accompanied by songs and chants in rhythm with the bouncing of the ball. These could be very intricate and complicated and usually involved the use of two or more old tennis balls. I was fine with two and could do as well as anyone, but when it came to playing with three, I'm afraid my hand/eye co-ordination let me down and I never mastered the art of what was, to all intents and purposes, a simple form of juggling.

I don't recall many girls playing conkers either, but I loved collecting them from under the trees in the Park. It was like magic to split the prickly green outer casing open and find the beautiful, shiny brown nut inside. We used to collect the conkers, take them to school and with Miss Leppard's help, pierce them and string them into long lines that were wound round the pillars in the church as decoration for Harvest Festival and very beautiful they looked too.

I loved playing Hop Scotch, which was a game that appealed in many ways, because it could be played alone as well as with other girls (boys didn't play it), no equipment was required, except a piece of chalk and a concrete path or paving stones to draw on. Chalk stones could be picked up with ease from any of the fields we played near and this was tougher and better than the fancy sticks of chalk we used to draw on our black boards.

I loved skipping in the playground and the more girls there were the better. Although skipping alone could be done at home or along the lane, the social skipping with a long rope was the best. Someone would bring in a length of good heavy rope (cart rope we called it), which was better than any of the flimsy toy skipping ropes available to us and we would then take it in turns to 'turn', while the others skipped. Good turners were essential for the game to be a success. Not every girl had this skill, but if you had two experts at either end of the rope, then it could be an exhilarating experience. There were strict rules and if you were 'out', which meant you didn't let the rope pass cleanly beneath your feet as you jumped, then you had to stand patiently and wait until every girl had skipped, or turn the rope for the others, then you could try again.

The more skilled among us loved to perform what we called 'bumps', which meant we jumped once, while the rope passed under our feet twice. This entailed good timing and rhythm and expert rope turning.

Some girls could do this whilst skipping alone and turning the rope themselves, but I never mastered that art, always preferring someone else to turn for me.

All skipping games were accompanied by songs and chants. I can recall one that was popular when we did bumps. All the words accompanied single jumps, except the last in each line, when we would emphasise it and perform a 'bump'. It went like this.

A house to LET,
No rent to PAY,
Knock at the DOOR,
And run AWAY,

This was followed by the same verse sung again, but with each word accentuated by a bump.

There was another.

Jumbo, Jumbo, sitting on a rainbow,
Eating mouldy cheese HA HA!
When a long came a copper,
Hit him on his topper,
Which made poor Jumbo sneeze HA HA!

Most of the song was sung as we skipped very quickly, with bumps on the 'Ha ha' words, then once again the verse was repeated with every word punctuated by a bump.

A popular skipping game was performed to the same rhyme that we said as we counted our plum or cherry stones, using them as a sort of fortune telling device.

As we skipped we chanted:

Tinker, tailor, soldier, sailor, rich man, poor man, beggar-man, thief.

Whichever of these we were 'out' on, indicated the job of our future husband. This was followed by whether our wedding dress would be, Silk, satin, muslin, rag, and whether our wedding ring would be gold, silver, copper or tin. There were other lists, too endless to record here.

If there were a lot of girls playing and we had a long enough rope, the turners would turn the rope quite slowly and we would chant, as we all ran in to skip 'All in together girls', the words of which I can't remember now, except I recall that at first the skipping was quite slow and sedate, but at the end we sang.

'Salt, Mustard, vinegar, PEPPER,'

The last word was the signal for the turners to turn the rope really quickly, until we were all skipping at a frantic pace until everyone was eventually out.

At the village school we played (under teacher supervision) a rather tame game called Over The Sun and Under The Moon.

The long rope was turned slowly and the children had to run under it one way across the playground and over it, as we ran back. Any child who got caught in the rope and caused it to stop turning was out. This was usually followed by a gentle game, which required the turners to swing the rope gently from side to side without it being turned, we would then jump from one side to the other chanting:

Bluebells, cockle shells, Evie, Ivy, over.

On the word 'over' the rope was turned and we had to skip one step and then jump out without stopping the rope.

The mysterious thing about playground games was that they appeared to be seasonal and the unwritten rules were strictly abided by. So one day we would all be playing ball games, then suddenly it was all change and all one could see was skipping ropes, then they were put away and everyone joined in with the catching games. No one seemed to decide that a change was due, it just seemed to happen... a sort of etiquette that we obeyed.

Cowboys and Indians was a very popular game outside of school hours and both girls and boys joined in with this, as we galloped round on our imaginary horses, shooting the baddies with wooden guns, or quite often with just pointed fingers. There were a few variations on this theme, depending on our reading matter. I recall that Cavaliers and Roundheads was popular for a time after Miss Leppard read Children of the New Forest to us. This stirring tale by Captain Marriott stirred our imaginations and made us long to be Royalist's or Cromwell's men.

Our knowledge of the American West came to us strictly from Hollywood, for we weren't taught about it in history lessons, so to us the Indians were the baddies and the clean-cut heroes were the cowboys. We knew nothing of the ill-treatment and abuse of the Native American in those days, we believed what we saw on the silver screen!

The boys also loved to play war games and would zoom around with out-stretched arms, pretending to be fighter planes, noisily shooting down the 'Jerries' or 'Japs' . We were all fed a diet of propaganda about the wicked enemy and the newspapers and new reels at the cinema were full of stories about battles that were won or lost, so it wasn't surprising that these things entered our games.

As a family we played the usual board games like Snakes & Ladders, Ludo and Monopoly and we like the simple card games like Old Maid, Beat Your Neighbour, Newmarket, and Rummy, but my particular favourite was a word game called Lexicon, which was similar to Scrabble, I think, but played with cards. I have to say I hated Snap and Happy Families and found them boring in the extreme.

Girls also liked to perform something we called 'Twizzles', to do this we stood face to face with their toes touching, we then crossed our arms and linked hands, leaned back as far as we could, until our arms were straight and begin to rotate, slowly at first, but increasing speed until we were spinning round rapidly. This became exhilarating as one's skirt flew out and the world flashed by as we whirled round and round. One had to have a lot of faith in one's partner, because if hands came unclasped, then one could fly off at a tangent and fall causing grazing to knees and elbows or worse. Boys wouldn't be seen dead playing this ... it would have been thought of as very 'sissy'!

We used to love playing a game that we called Mr. Fish. A child was selected by one of the many rituals we used to decide who was 'It'. This was usually an elimination chant, when all the children wanting to play stood in a ring with hands (in a fist) stretched out. The leader would then touch each fist as he/she chanted;

'A penn'orth of chips to grease your lips, O.U.T. spells out.', the child whose hand was touched as the last letter was spoken was out and the ritual was repeated until only one child remained, this child was the Boss-child (or 'It') for the next game.

In Mr. Fish, the Boss-child stood at one end of the playground, with all the other children lined up at the other. They would then call in unison,

"Please, Mr. Fish, may we cross over your water?"

The Boss-child would answer,

"Not unless you are wearing blue/ have brown eyes, have freckles etc, etc." whatever he/she chose.

The children who qualified were allowed to cross over unmolested, then the others, at a given signal, had to make a run for it and try to gain the other side of the playground without being caught by Mr. Fish and his helpers. The child remaining un-caught then became Mr. Fish for the next game. This game gave plenty of scope for cheating, because Mr. Fish could make sure his friends qualified for crossing safely!

Another favourite was a game we called Statues. This en-tailed the Boss-child taking the hand of each child in turn, pulling them into a tight circle and suddenly letting go. The child then had to stay perfectly still in the position that they landed. Any child who moved before every child was pulled out, was dis-missed from the game. The last child to move was the 'It' for the next game. One could assume many bizarre positions when playing this game and it was then that fits of giggles caused one to move!

Young girls love to dress up and we usually became beautiful 'brides', when a bit of old lace curtain and a bunch of wilting wild flowers transformed us into something very glamorous indeed. The game was even better if we could persuade a willing boy to join in and became our 'bridegroom', but they soon became bored and wanted to go off and play with other boys. During one of the 'wedding' games I married John Lovell and thereafter we would go to each others birthday parties and play kissing games like Postman's Knock. He was about nine and I was eight. I still see John occasionally and remind him of this! Gill Curtis once married Keith Stukins in a similar ceremony, even though he was more than a year younger than her. Was he the first Toy-Boy, I wonder!

My friend Jean Cox and I didn't play any of these traditional or organised games, but preferred to make up games and sce-narios of our own. We were often glamorous cowgirls of the Wild West, based on our only knowledge of them, which was gained via the movies we occasionally saw. We pretended to be Holly-wood beauties like Rhonda Fleming, Virginia Mayo and the like, clad in imaginary fringed buckskin clothes and mounted on equally imaginary thoroughbred horses, as we galloped round Jean's cottage at the end of Owls End, pretending it was the wide open prairie.

Jean and I also enacted stories based on our favourite characters in the magazine, Girls Crystal, that she subscribed to. There were always tales of the exploits of a quartet of youngsters called Sally and Faye and their (strictly platonic) respective boyfriends Don and Dick. Sally was pretty, with dark curly hair and Faye (equally as pretty) wore her hair in a blonde page-boy bob. Jean chose to be Sally (it was her magazine, so she had the right to be who she wanted to be!) and I was Faye. We played for hours in the persona of these girls and acted out quite complicated stories.

I don't ever recall Jean and I playing any of the traditional games. We preferred to be imaginative and act out tales of adventure and romance.

We were also devoted to the entertainer George Formby and her Dad would sometimes take us to Huntingdon (on our bikes) to see a film in which he starred. We both longed for a ukulele for Christmas. I did get a toy plastic one, but I think I am right in saying that Jean was given a real instrument. I don't know if she learned to play it or not. I could only get a metallic, tuneless noise out of mine!

What's The Time, Mr. Wolf?, Grandmother's Footsteps and the like are still played today, which is amazing, when you think that the era I am writing about is more than sixty years ago and I am sure a lot of the games were played by generations of children long before that, yet they have all been passed down, mostly by word of mouth, with very little change. Long may it continue to be that way.

FINAL WORDS

I sincerely hope that whoever reads this book has enjoyed sharing my memories of a childhood spent in an age long ago. Times were hard and we were poor, but since most people were in the same boat and no one told us we were deprived, we were more or less happy with our lot.

In writing these memoirs I have tried to be honest to the best of my ability, but I beg forgiveness for any errors found and ask you to remember these are the memories of a child and recorded as I remember them happening at the time.

If I have been unkind to a few villagers, then that is the way I saw things at the time. A child sees things in black and white when in reality they are often in many shades of grey. If I have offended anyone (or their descendants) then I apologise and ask for forgiveness and tolerance. No malice was intended.

Although it is almost fifty years since I lived in Great Stukeley, it will always remain in my memory as a place where I was happy and contented. The people I knew were on the whole, honest and hard working. Our lives were more or less serene in spite of the war, rationing, lack of facilities and money.

I will never forget the characters who shared my world and if this book helps to keep their memory alive then it has been worthwhile.